Qaṭf al-Azhār

HARVESTING SCATTERED FLOWERS

بسم الله الرحمن الرحيم

Qaṭf al-Azhār

HARVESTING SCATTERED FLOWERS

A Collection of Mass-Transmitted Hadiths

IMAM JALĀL AD-DĪN AS-SUYŪṬĪ

(D. 911/1505)

Translated by

NASIR ABDUSSALAM

Edited by

SHOAIB SHAH AND SAJJAD SHAH

TURATH PUBLISHING

ISBN: 978-1-906949-53-2

Published by:
Turath Publishing
79 Mitcham Road London SW17 9PD
www.turath.co.uk +44 (20) 8767 3666

Author Imam Jalāl ad-Dīn as-Suyūṭī
Translation Nasir Abdussalam
Editor Shoaib Shah & Sajjad Shah
Final Editor Mariam Madge Conlan
General Editor Yahya Batha

British Library Cataloguing in Publication Data
As-Suyūṭī Imam Jalāl ad-Dīn
Qatf al-Azhār – A Collection of Mass-Transmitted Hadiths
I. Title

Design & typesetting ARM (www.whitethreadpress.com)
Printed by Mega Printers, Istanbul

Distributors for UK and Europe
Azhar Academy Ltd.
54–56 Little Ilford Lane, London E12 5QA
trade@azharacademy.com
www.azharacademy.com

Distributors for South Africa
Darul-Ihsan Research and Education Centre
www.darulihsan.com

الْإِسْنَادُ مِنَ الدِّينِ
لَوْلَا الْإِسْنَادُ لَقَالَ مَنْ شَاءَ مَا شَاءَ

ʿAbdullāh ibn al-Mubārak said,

'*Isnād* is from the *dīn*. Were it not for *isnād*,

anyone would say anything he likes.'

(*Muqaddamah Ibn Ṣalāḥ*, p. 256)

Contents

Publisher's Foreword

IN THE NAME OF ALLAH, the Most Merciful and Compassionate. I bear witness that there is no god but Allah alone, without partners, and that Muḥammad ﷺ is His servant and Messenger. I invoke the blessings of Allah and peace upon His final Messenger, Muḥammad, his family, Companions and all those who follow them in goodness till the Day of Rising.

The mass-transmitted (*mutawātir*) hadith is a source of highly authenticated sacred knowledge and as such deserves our profound attention in an age in which the plethora of opinions available to the layman can be a source of confusion and even doubt. Imam Bazdawī[1] defines the *mutawātir* as a report 'that reaches you from the Messenger of Allah ﷺ via a transmission containing no doubt, such that it is as if you hear it from an eyewitness. This is due to its great number of narrators whose collusion cannot be countenanced, owing to their uprightness and clearly different locations.'

Leaving aside any disagreement regarding exactly which hadith can be classified as *mutawātir*, the essential point to grasp is that the information contained in hadith which have been transmitted by numerous respected narrators simply cannot be disregarded. As such, they provide an antidote to the malady of looking for loopholes which modern society with all its peer pressure would have us succumb to.

Imam Suyūṭī, may Allah reward him, considered the hadith in this collection to be *mutawātir*. Not only this, he recognised the mani-

1 *Kashf al-Asrār*, 2:360.

fold benefits for the layman of having awareness of these anchors of certainty that touch on a wide range of the fundamental principles and practices of Islam, so much so that he reduced and simplified a larger work of his on the same topic specifically for a wider audience. When this was the case historically, surely it is all the more so for us today, when the authenticity of the whole hadith corpus has come under attack, including sources of dogma (*ʿaqīdah*). We pray that the Imam's worthy aspiration comes to fruition for our generation and generations to come through the efforts of all those who have worked on this translation.

All praise if for Allah. Thereafter, I would like to thank Nasir Abdussalam for his erudite translation. Thanks also to Mawlānā Shoaib Shah and his brother Sajjad Shah for their careful and insightful editing, and to Mariam Madge Conlan for bringing the work to its final format. Finally, we are especially grateful to HRH Prince Ghazi who had also begun work on a version of this valuable text but generously sent over his translation for us to benefit from, may Allah reward his sincerity. I pray that Allah accepts the efforts of all involved and makes it a means for our forgiveness and a source of benefit and certainty for all those who read it. May He raise us on the Day of Judgement with those whom he has forgiven totally and enter us into the Garden with our beloved Prophet ﷺ, along with our family, teachers and friends. Ameen.

YAHYA BATHA
London 2019

Translator's Introduction

IN THE NAME OF ALLAH, the Beneficent, the Merciful. All praise is to Allah, and may Allah bless and give peace to our Master, Muḥammad, his family, his Companions and all those who follow them in excellence until the Day of Recompense.

The content of this work by the great 10th century Egyptian polymath, Jalāl ad-Dīn as-Suyūṭī ﷺ, is of a value that defies its small size. It is a very rare type of hadith collection dedicated to an even rarer type of hadith—the mass-transmitted. The mass-transmitted report is one in which a piece of information is corroborated by a multitude of eyewitnesses whose relative abundance (in accordance with common experience) precludes a conspiracy to lie, and is continuously transmitted by similar multitudes from the original witnesses to the present. One of the salient qualities of Islam is its concern with certainty in regards to establishing the fundamentals of the religion. The mass-transmitted report is a means of acquiring certainty (as opposed to probability), along with sound senses and reason.

For example, despite never having been to Mexico, I am certain that Mexico exists. Why? Because in my lifetime, I have heard of its existence from a countless number of people who are actually from or have been there, and according to my knowledge of normal human behavior, I know that it is practically impossible for all of them to have conspired to make up a country called Mexico. Likewise, despite never having met Julius Caesar personally, I am certain that he existed and certain of who he was. This is because the number of those who did know him is so great; it is impossible that they conspired to make up such a public figure and passed along that false information to the succeeding generation (and that generation to the next, and so and on and so forth until now).

Mass-transmitted reports concerning the words, deeds, or tacit approvals of the Prophet Muḥammad ﷺ are indeed rare, especially when compared to the thousands upon thousands of solitary reports (i.e. reports originally transmitted by just one, a couple or a few witnesses) dealing with the same information. Mass-transmitted reports are divided into two categories: verbatim, which is exceptionally rare; or a report that indicates a general meaning, which the bulk of mass-transmitted reports are.

This poor slave of Allah has attempted something of a brief annotation for some of the hadiths in order to clarify the meaning when necessary, or to provide some benefit to the reader where appropriate. I have also added *takhrīj* where the full reference has not been given or where the hadith appears elsewhere. There are 113 hadiths in Imam Suyūṭī's ﵀ collection, some of which he did not actually relate the wording for due to them being so well known. In these instances, I have added the actual hadith. May Allah ﷻ reward Suyūṭī ﵀ for this great work, and place this English rendering in both his and my scale of good deeds.

Author's Introduction

ALL PRAISE IS TO ALLAH for His continuous blessings. I testify that there is no god except Allah, alone, and that He has no associate—a testimony that He has made the means of salvation from the horrors of the next life. And I testify that Muḥammad is His slave and Messenger; may Allah bless him, his family, his Companions and whoever supports and assists him.

To proceed: I authored a book entitled *Al-Fawāʾid al-Mutakaththirah fiʾ l-Akhbār al-Mutawātirah* (*The Manifold Benefits of Mass-Transmitted Hadiths*), mentioning therein what ten or more Companions have related, and including all the paths of transmission and variant wordings of each hadith.[1] It ended up being a huge work, like nothing done

---

1 Traditionally, scholars would introduce the student of each science to the 'ten principles' of that science (*al-mabādiʾ al-ʿasharah*)—its definition, subject, founder, end, issues, name, relation, value, ruling and source. This work of Suyūṭī's ﷺ deals with the science of hadith narration (*ʿilm al-ḥadīth riwāyatan*), whose ten elements are as follows:

- The definition—a science that consists of transmitting whatever was related to the Prophet ﷺ, whether word, deed, tacit approval or attribute.
- The subject—the person of the Prophet ﷺ insofar as he was a prophet (as opposed to an ordinary person).
- The founder—the Companions of the Prophet ﷺ, who undertook preserving his words, deeds, tacit approvals and attributes/description.
- The end result—acquiring good fortune in this world and the afterlife.
- The issues—all matters that fall under the Prophet's ﷺ teachings or example.
- The name—the science of hadith narration.
- The relation to other sciences—it is one of the revealed sciences (which are jurisprudence, Qur'anic exegesis and hadith).
- The value—it is of immense worth insofar as through it how to follow the Prophet ﷺ is known.
- The ruling—an individual obligation to a lone narrator (of critical information pertaining to a religious obligation); otherwise it is a collective obligation.

before it. However, due to the abundance of information within it, only those with a profound interest in hadith and lofty aspirations desire to read it, and how few those are! I therefore decided it was appropriate to extract its main points for inclusion in this much smaller book, so that a broader readership might benefit from it.

I mention the hadith and a number of the Companions ﷺ who related it, along with its attribution to those of the famous scholars who recorded it. This is enough to satisfy those seeking benefit. I have entitled this work *Harvesting Scattered Flowers: A Collection of Mass-Transmitted Hadiths* and have organised it in the same chapters as the original work.

- The source—the words, deeds, tacit approvals and attributes of the Prophet ﷺ.

The Book of Knowledge

١ - مَنْ كَذَبَ عَلَيَّ فَلْيَتَبَوَّأْ مَقْعَدَهُ مِنَ النَّارِ.

1. 'Whoever deliberately lies about me, let him take his seat in the Fire.'[1]

	Narrator	*Compiler(s)*
1	ʿAlī ibn Abī Ṭālib	Būkhārī (106) and Muslim (1)
2	Abū Hurayrah	Būkhārī (110) and Muslim (3)
3	Anas ibn Mālik	Būkhārī (108) and Muslim (2)
4	Mughīrah ibn Shuʿbah	Būkhārī (1291) and Muslim (4)
5	Zubayr ibn al-ʿAwwām	Būkhārī (107)
6	Salamah ibn al-Akwaʿ	Būkhārī (109)
7	Ibn ʿAmr	Būkhārī (3461)
8	Ibn Masʿūd	Tirmidhī (2257), Nasā'ī (4084)[2] and Ibn Mājah (30)
9	Jābir ibn ʿAbdillāh	Ibn Mājah (33)
10	Abū Qatādah	Ibn Mājah (35)
11	Abū Saʿīd al-Khudrī	Ibn Mājah (37)
12	ʿAmmār ibn Ḥabīb	Ḥākim
13	Yaʿlā ibn Murrah	Dārimī (240)
14	ʿUmar ibn al-Khaṭṭāb	Aḥmad (326)
15	ʿUthmān ibn ʿAffān	Aḥmad (469)

1 The Sunnah of the Prophet ﷺ is divine revelation—'*He does not speak from his own desire*' (Qur'an 53:3). His function as Allah's Messenger was to deliver Allah's Message, so to lie about him ﷺ is essentially to lie about Allah ﷻ.

2 Found in Nasā'ī's *As-Sunan al-Kubrā*. There is no mention of Ibn Masʿūd. There is, however, an unspecified mention of a Companion of the Prophet ﷺ.

16	Khālid ibn ʿUrfuṭah	Aḥmad (22501)
17	Zayd ibn Arqam	Aḥmad (19266)
18	Ibn ʿUmar	Aḥmad (4742)
19	ʿUqbah ibn ʿĀmir	Aḥmad (17431)
20	Qays ibn Saʿd	Aḥmad (15482)
21	Muʿāwiyah ibn Abī Sufyān	Aḥmad (16830)
22	Abū Saʿīd al-Khudrī	Aḥmad (11092)
23	Abū Mūsā al-Ghāfiqī	Aḥmad (18946)
24	Abū Bakr aṣ-Ṣiddīq	Ṭabarānī, *Awsaṭ* (2838)
25	Ṭalḥah ibn ʿAbdillāh	Ṭabarānī, *Kabīr* (204)
26	Aws ibn Aws	Ṭabarānī, *Kabīr* (591)
27	Barāʾ ibn ʿĀzib	Ṭabarānī, *Awsaṭ* (8183)
28	Ḥudhayfah ibn al-Yamān	Ṭabarānī, *Awsaṭ* (5607)
29	Rāfiʿ ibn Khadīj	Ṭabarānī, *Kabīr* (4410)
30	Sāʾib ibn Yazīd	Ṭabarānī, *Kabīr* (6679)
31	Saʿd ibn al-Midḥās	Ṭabarānī, *Kabīr* (5502)
32	Salmān al-Fārisī	Ṭabarānī, *Kabīr* (6163)
33	Ṣuhayb	Ṭabarānī, *Kabīr* (7302)
34	Ibn ʿAbbās	Ṭabarānī, *Kabīr* (12392)
35	ʿUtbah ibn Ghazwān	Ṭabarānī, *Kabīr* (288)
36	ʿUrs ibn ʿUmayr[1]	Ṭabarānī, *Kabīr* (346)
37	ʿAmmār ibn Yāsir	Ṭabarānī, *Ṭuruq Ḥadīth man Kadhab* (49)
38	ʿAmr ibn Ḥurayth	Ṭabarānī, *Ṭuruq Ḥadīth man Kadhab* (138)
39	ʿAmr ibn ʿAbasah	Ṭabarānī, *Ṭuruq Ḥadīth man Kadhab* (139)
40	ʿAmr ibn Murrah	Ṭabarānī, *Awsaṭ* (3686)
41	Muʿādh ibn Jabal	Ṭabarānī, *Awsaṭ* (1202)
42	Nubayṭ ibn Sharīṭ	Ṭabarānī, *Awsaṭ* (67)
43	Yaʿlā ibn Murrah	Ṭabarānī, *Ṭuruq Ḥadīth man Kadhaba* (153)

1 Ṭabarānī has ʿUrs ibn ʿUmayrah.

44	Abū Umāmah	Ṭabarānī, *Kabīr* (7557)
45	Abū Mūsā al-Ashʿarī	Ṭabarānī, *Awsaṭ* (5759)
46	Abū Maymūn al-Kurdī	Ṭabarānī, *Awsaṭ* (6213)
47	Abū Qirṣāfah	Ṭabarānī, *Kabīr* (2516)
48	The father of Abū Mālik al-Ashjaʿī whose name is Ṭāriq ibn Ashyam	Ṭabarānī, *Kabīr* (8181)
49	Saʿīd ibn Zayd	Bazzār, *Musnad* (1275)
50	ʿImrān ibn Ḥuṣayn	Bazzār, *Musnad* (3612)
51	Salmān al-Fārisī	Dāraquṭnī, *Afrād*[1]
52	Ibn az-Zubayr	Dāraquṭnī, *Afrād*
53	Yazīd ibn Asad	Dāraquṭnī, *Afrād*[2]
54	Abū Rimthah	Dāraquṭnī, *Afrād*[3]
55	Abū Rāfiʿ	Dāraquṭnī, *ʿIlal* (7:47)
56	Umm Ayman	Dāraquṭnī, *Afrād*[4]
57	Jābir	Abū Nuʿaym, *Ḥilyah* (9:59)
58	Jābir ibn Ḥābis	Abū Nuʿaym[5]
59	Salmān ibn Khālid	Abū Nuʿaym[6]
60	ʿAbdullāh ibn Zughb	Abū Nuʿaym[7]
61	Mughīrah ibn Shuʿbah	Abū Nuʿaym, *Al-Musnad al-Mustakhraj ʿalā Ṣaḥīḥ Muslim* (66)
62	Usāmah ibn Yazīd	Ibn Qāniʿ, *Muʿjam aṣ-Ṣahābah*[8]
63	ʿAbdullāh ibn Abī Awfā	Ibn Qāniʿ, *Muʿjam aṣ-Ṣahābah*[9]
64	Buraydah	Ibn ʿAdī, *Kāmil*[10]

1 Ṭabarānī, *Kabīr* (6163).
2 Ibn ʿAsākir (2469).
3 Muttaqī al-Hindī, *Kanz* (8238).
4 Ibid.
5 Ṭabarānī, *Ṭuruq Ḥadīth man Kadhab* (174).
6 Muttaqī al-Hindī, *Kanz* (8238).
7 Ṭabarānī, *Ṭuruq Ḥadīth man Kadhab* (170).
8 I could not find this hadith. Ṭabarānī records the same hadith from Usāmah ibn Zayd (*Kabīr* 426).
9 ʿIrāqī, Ibn as-Subkī and Zubaydī, *Takhrīj Aḥādīth Iḥyā'* (115).
10 Ṭabarānī, *Ṭuruq Ḥadīth man Kadhab* (146).

65	Safīnah	Ibn ʿAdī, *Kāmil*[1]
66	Wāthilah ibn al-Asqaʿ	Ibn ʿAdī, *Kāmil*
67	Abū ʿUbaydah ibn al-Jarrāh	Khaṭīb, *Tārīkh* (3434)
68	Saʿd ibn Abī Waqqāṣ	Khaṭīb, *Tārīkh* (609)
69	Ḥudhayfah ibn Asīd	Khaṭīb, *Tārīkh*[2]
70	Zayd ibn Thābit	Khaṭīb, *Tārīkh*
71	Kaʿb ibn Quṭbah	Khaṭīb, *Tārīkh*[3]
72	Muʿāwiyah ibn Ḥaydah	Khaṭīb, *Tārīkh* (1362)
73	Munaqqaʿ at-Tamīmī	Khaṭīb, *Tārīkh*[4]
74	Abū Kabshah al-Anṣārī	Khaṭīb, *Tārīkh* (4004)
75	The father of Abū' l-ʿUsharā'	Khaṭīb, *Tārīkh*
76	Abū Dharr	Khaṭīb, *Tārīkh*[5]
77	ʿĀ'ishah	Khaṭīb, *Tārīkh*[6]

The following are also mentioned among the narrators of this hadith:

78 ʿAbd ar-Raḥmān ibn ʿAwf[7]
79 ʿAmr ibn ʿAwf[8]
80 Abu 'l-Ḥamrā'

٢ - نَضَّرَ اللَّهُ عَبْدًا سَمِعَ مَقَالَتِي فَوَعَاهَا فَأَدَّاهَا إِلَى مَنْ لَمْ يَسْمَعْهَا، فَرُبَّ حَامِلِ فِقْهٍ لَا فِقْهَ لَهُ، وَرُبَّ حَامِلِ فِقْهٍ إِلَى مَنْ هُوَ أَفْقَهُ مِنْهُ.

2. 'Allah illuminates the person who hears a statement of mine,

1 Ibn al-Muqri' in his *Muʿjam* (190).

2 Suyūṭī, *Al-Fatḥ al-Kabīr* (12279).

3 Ṭabarānī, *Ṭuruq Ḥadīth man Kadhab* (173).

4 Ṭabarānī in *Kabīr* has recorded a different hadith wherein Munaqqaʿ informed the Prophet ﷺ of what people were saying and he ﷺ responded, 'O Allah, it is not lawful for them to lie about me.' (712)

5 Ṭabarānī in *Ṭuruq Ḥadīth man Kadhab* (171).

6 Ṭaḥāwī, *Sharḥ Mushkil* (394).

7 Ibn al-Jawzī said that he has not come across this hadith from ʿAbd ar-Raḥmān ibn ʿAwf. (Laknawī, *Al-Āthār al-Marfūʿah*, p.35)

8 Abū Ḥudhayfah Nabīl ibn Manṣūr has quoted it in *Anīs as-Sārī* (10:90).

memorises it and shares it with those who have not heard it. Perhaps the carrier of knowledge does not understand, or perhaps he [understands yet] carries it to someone with more understanding.'[1]

1 This hadith illustrates the very important distinction between the preservation and transmission of hadith versus the understanding of hadith needed to derive legal rulings. Unfortunately, this critical difference between the sciences of hadith and the science of jurisprudence and its principles is lost on many Muslims today. Of the approximately 140,000 Companions, fatwas from about 130 are preserved, and of these 130 only seven were prolific: ʿUmar ibn al-Khaṭṭāb, ʿAlī ibn Abī Ṭālib, ʿAbdullāh ibn Masʿūd, Zayd ibn Thābit, ʿAbdullāh ibn ʿAbbās, ʿAbdullāh ibn ʿUmar, and ʿĀ'ishah bint Abī Bakr ﷺ. Though some of the aforementioned were also prolific narrators of hadith, like ʿĀ'ishah ﷺ, others of the most prolific narrators of hadith such as Abū Hurayrah ﷺ were not known for giving fatwas; however, legal rulings were most definitely derived from what they narrated by the Imams of the Successors (*Tābiʿīn*).

As a matter of fact, the sciences of hadith were initially a field within legal theory, seeing as how knowledge of narrators and what is permissible to adduce and derive rulings from is a prerequisite for being an independent *mujtahid* [i.e. a legist qualified to formulate independent rulings]. Furthermore, not every sound hadith is acted upon by every independent *mujtahid*, due to other considerations that the given *mujtahid* views as sound according to his principles. Examples of this can be found in the earliest extant work of hadith available to us, the *Muwaṭṭa'* of Imām Mālik ﷺ. Therein he narrates a number of sound hadiths on issues for which his fatwa is at variance, due to his principle of giving priority to the practice of Medīnan scholars.

There are five levels of *mujtahid*: the independent *mujtahid*, such as Imams Abū Ḥanīfah, Mālik, Shāfiʿī and Aḥmad; the *mujtahid* nominally ascribed to an Imam, such as Muzanī (who is nominally ascribed to Shāfiʿī); the *mujtahid* of a school, such as Qaffāl ash-Shāshī; the *mujtahid* of fatwa, such as Nawawī; and the transmitter, such as Ibn Ḥajar al-Haytamī.

The prerequisites of an independent *mujtahid* are that he know the evidences of legal rulings from the Qur'an, the Sunnah, scholarly consensus and analogy in detail (i.e. how and from what perspectives they may be adduced), as well as having his own unique principles for adducing said evidences. Thus, he must be knowledgeable of the exegesis of Qur'anic verses pertaining to legal rulings, knowledgeable of the chains of narration for hadiths pertaining to legal rulings, knowledgeable of the abrogating and abrogated from these sources and proficient in Arabic grammar and lexicology. The *mujtahid* nominally ascribed to an Imam is like the independent *mujtahid*, but has a nominal ascription due to the overall concurrence of his principles with the principles of the independent *mujtahid*. The *mujtahid* of a school is restricted to the principles of his Imam and capable of establishing them with their proofs. His mastery of his Imam's principles enables him to derive rulings on issues that his Imam did not give a fatwa on. The *mujtahid* of fatwa is proficient in the principles of his school and a master of the divergent fatwas within it and their respective evidences. Through this mastery, he is capable of evaluating fatwas within the school and discerning the sound from the weak. The transmitter possesses mastery of the divergent fatwas of the school and understands their evidences, but not

In many paths of its transmission is the additional wording: 'There are three things for which the heart of the believer is never bitter—making works purely for the sake of Allah, obedience to those in authority and adhering to the group.'

	Narrator	*Compiler(s)*
1	Zayd ibn Thābit	Tirmidhī (2656), Nasā'ī, *As-Sunan al-Kubrā* (5816), Ibn Mājah (230) and Abū Dāwūd (3660)
2	Ibn Masʿūd	Tirmidhī (2657)
3	Jubayr ibn Muṭʿim	Ḥākim (294)
4	Nuʿmān ibn Bashīr	Ḥākim (297)
5	Saʿd ibn Abī Waqqāṣ	Ṭabarānī, *Awsaṭ* (7020)
6	Anas	Ṭabarānī, *Awsaṭ* (9444)
7	Bashīr (father of Nuʿmān)	Ṭabarānī
8	Jābir ibn ʿAbdillāh	Ṭabarānī, *Awsaṭ* (5292)
9	ʿUmayr ibn Qatādah al-Laythī	Ṭabarānī, *Awsaṭ* (7004)
10	Muʿādh ibn Jabal	Ṭabarānī, *Awsaṭ* (6781)

---

to the degree of mastery possessed by the *mujtahid* of fatwa. Therefore, he is not capable of evaluating fatwas; however, he is capable of giving fatwas on new issues by drawing analogies to the wealth of fatwas he has learned within his school.

Imam Nawawī ﷺ states in the introduction to *Majmūʿ*:

These are the types of muftis, which are five. Every type among them has the prerequisite of memorising the school and natural intelligence. Whoever undertakes giving fatwas and is not of this description has brought upon himself something tremendous.

The Seal of the Verifying Imams of the *Shāfiʿī*s, Ibn Ḥajar al-Haytami ﷺ, states in *Al-Fatāwā al-Kubrā*:

This status is not achieved easily, nor are its high walls breached by whoever memorises and dabbles in some derivative issues without guidance to their understanding, without knowing their source and without knowing what is said about them. Breaching that prohibitive wall is only possible for he who has delved into a plethora of jurisprudence until it mixes with his flesh and blood, and has become legally keen by second-nature, to the extent that if he judges with his opinion on an issue whose transmission he is not privy to, he would find that what he judges was said previously by one of the scholars. When jurisprudence is firmly grounded within him until he reaches this level, then he is permitted to issue fatwas. As for before he reaches this level, then it is not allowed for him to give fatwas. His only job is to be quiet about what does not concern him and refer to the experts, for it is a field that does not accept intrusion, and no one reaches its broad parameters except one whom his Master has blessed with extensive success and grace.

11	Abu ad-Dardā'	Ṭabarānī[1]
12	Abū Qirṣāfah	Ṭabarānī, *Awsaṭ* (3072)
13	Abū Sa'īd al-Khudrī	Bazzār[2]
14	Rabī'ah ibn Uthmān at-Taymī	Abū Nu'aym[3]
15	Ibn 'Umar	Rāfi'ī, *Tārīkh Qazwīn*[4]
16	Zayd ibn Khālid al-Juhanī	Ibn 'Asākir, *Tārīkh* (2522)

1 Dārimī (236).

2 Ṭabarānī, *Musnad as-Shāmiyyīn* (1302).

3 Ibn Kathīr, *Jāmi' al-Masānīd wa 's-Sunan* (3027).

4 Ṭabarānī, *Musnad as-Shāmiyyīn* (508).

The Book of Faith

٣ - مَنْ شَهِدَ أَنْ لَا إِلَهَ إِلَّا اللهُ وَجَبَتْ لَهُ الْجَنَّةُ.

3. 'Paradise is incumbent upon anyone who testifies that there is no god except Allah.'

	Narrator	*Compiler(s)*
1	Muʿādh ibn Jabal	Būkhārī (128) and Muslim (32)[1]
2	ʿUthmān ibn Mālik[2]	Būkhārī (425) and Muslim (33)
3	Abū Dharr	Būkhārī (6443) and Muslim (94)
4	ʿUthmān ibn ʿAffān	Būkhārī and Muslim (26)
5	ʿUbādah ibn aṣ-Ṣāmit	Muslim (47) and Aḥmad (22711)
6	Abū Hurayrah	Ibn Ḥibbān (6466)
7	Abū Bakr	Aḥmad[3]
8	ʿUmar	Aḥmad[4]
9	Khuzaym ibn Fātik[5]	Aḥmad (19035)
10	Rifāʿah al-Juhanī	Aḥmad (16218)
11	Salamah ibn Nuʿaym al-Ashjaʿī	Aḥmad[6]
12	Sahl ibn Bayḍā'[7]	Aḥmad (15738)
13	Shaddād ibn Aws	Aḥmad (17121)
14	Ibn ʿAmr	Aḥmad

1 Anas ibn Mālik relates the hadith about Muʿādh.
2 Bukhārī, Muslim and others have ʿItbān ibn Mālik.
3 Ṭabarānī, *Musnad as-Shāmiyyīn* (2258).
4 Ibn Ḥibbān (204).
5 Aḥmad has Khuraym ibn Fātik.
6 Ṭabarānī in *Awsaṭ* (2124).
7 Aḥmad has Suhayl ibn al-Bayḍā'.

15	Abu ad-Dardā'	Aḥmad (27491)
16	Abū Sa'īd al-Khudrī	Aḥmad (11000)
17	Abū 'Amrah al-Anṣārī	Aḥmad (15449)
18	Abū Mūsā al-Ash'arī	Aḥmad (19597)
19	Bilāl	Ṭabarānī, *Awsaṭ* (1123)
20	Jarīr ibn 'Abdillāh	Ṭabarānī[1]
21	Zayd ibn Arqam	Ṭabarānī, *Awsaṭ* (1235)
22	Zayd ibn Khālid al-Juhanī[2]	Ṭabarānī, *Kabīr* (5262)
23	Sa'd ibn 'Ubādah	Ṭabarānī, *Awsaṭ* (1364)
24	Ibn 'Abbās	Ṭabarānī, *Du'ā'* (1544)
25	Ibn 'Umar	Ṭabarānī, *Kabīr* (13595)
26	'Uqbah ibn 'Āmir	Ṭabarānī, *Du'ā'* (1460)
27	'Umārah ibn Ruwaybah	Ṭabarānī, *Awsaṭ* (405)
28	'Umar ibn Ḥuṣayn[3]	Ṭabarānī, *Kabīr* (253)
29	'Iyāḍ al-Anṣārī	Ṭabarānī[4]
30	Nawwās ibn Sam'ān	Ṭabarānī, *Musnad ash-Shāmiyyīn* (3522)
31	Abū Shaybah al-Khudrī	Ṭabarānī, *Awsaṭ* (2426)
32	'Abd ar-Raḥmān ibn 'Awf	Bazzār (1042)
33	Jābir ibn 'Abdillāh	Abū Ya'lā (1820)

٤ - أُمِرْتُ أَنْ أُقَاتِلَ النَّاسَ حَتَّى يَقُولُوا لاَ إِلَهَ إِلاَّ اللهُ.

4. 'I was commanded to fight people[5] until they say that there is no god except Allah.'

In many paths of its transmission is the additional wording: 'If they say it, then they have protected their blood and their wealth from

1 Aḥmad (14721).

2 Some variations have Abū Zayd ibn Khālid al-Juhanī.

3 This seems to be an error in the transcription. Ṭabarānī has recorded a variation of this hadith in the reference above from 'Imrān ibn Ḥuṣayn.

4 Haythamī, *Majma'* (55).

5 The people referred to in this hadith are Arab idolaters. The usage of 'people' here is an instance of a general wording with a specific intent.

me and their reckoning is with Allah, except in regard to what there is a prescribed punishment for.'

	Narrator	*Compiler(s)*
1	Jābir ibn ʿAbdillāh	Būkhārī and Muslim (21)[1]
2	Ibn ʿAmr[2]	Muslim (36)
3	Abū Hurayrah	Muslim (32)
4	Abū Bakr aṣ-Ṣiddīq	Ibn Abī Shaybah, *Mūsānnaf*[3]
5	ʿUmar	Ibn Abī Shaybah, *Mūsānnaf* (37054)
6	Ibn Uways ath-Thaqafī[4]	Ibn Abī Shaybah, *Mūsānnaf* (28937)
7	Jarīr ibn ʿAbdillāh al-Bajalī	Ibn Abī Shaybah, *Mūsānnaf* (28938)
8	Anas	Ṭabarānī, *Awsaṭ* (3221)
9	Samurah ibn Jundub	Ṭabarānī, *Awsaṭ* (6465)
10	Sahl ibn Saʿd	Ṭabarānī, *Kabīr* (5746)
11	Ibn ʿAbbās	Ṭabarānī, *Awsaṭ* (6923)
12	Abū Bakrah	Ṭabarānī, *Awsaṭ* (3625)
13	Abū Mālik al-Ashjaʿī (on the authority of his father, Ṭāriq ibn Ashyam)	Ṭabarānī, *Kabīr* (8191)
14	ʿĪyāḍ al-Anṣārī	Bazzār[5]
15	Nuʿmān ibn Bashīr	Bazzār (3227)

٥ - الْمُسْلِمُ مَنْ سَلِمَ الْمُسْلِمُونَ مِنْ لِسَانِهِ وَيَدِهِ.

5. 'The true Muslim is he from whose tongue and hands the Muslims are safe.'

1 ʿAbd ar-Razzāq, *Muṣannaf* (10021).

2 Muslim has Ibn ʿUmar.

3 Shāfiʿī relates this hadith from Abū Hurayrah who relates that ʿUmar quoted this statement from the Prophet ﷺ to Abū Bakr. Abū Bakr then replied, 'This [i.e. zakat] is a right of belief.' (*Musnad*, p.169.)

4 Ibn Abī Shaybah has Ibn Aws.

5 Haythamī in *Majmaʿ az-Zawāʾid* (55) has also related it from Bazzār.

	Narrator	Compiler(s)
1	ʿAbdullāh ibn ʿAmr ibn al-ʿĀṣ	Būkhārī (10) and Muslim (64)
2	Jābir ibn ʿAbdillāh	Muslim (65)
3	Abū Mūsā	Muslim (66)
4	Anas	Ḥākim (25)
5	Faḍālah ibn ʿUbayd	Ḥākim (24)
6	Abū Hurayrah	Ḥākim (22)
7	Muʿādh [ibn Anas]	Aḥmad (15635)
8	ʿAmr ibn ʿAbasah	Aḥmad (19435)
9	Bilāl ibn al-Ḥārith	Ṭabarānī, *Kabīr* (1137)
10	Ibn ʿUmar	Ṭabarānī[1]
11	Abū Umāmah	Ṭabarānī, *Kabīr* (8021)
12	Wāthilah ibn al-Asqaʿ	Ṭabarānī, *Kabīr* (193)
13	Nuʿmān ibn Bashīr	Ṭabarānī[2]

٦ - لا يَزْنِي الزَّانِي حِينَ يَزْنِي وَهُوَ مُؤْمِنٌ.

6. 'The fornicator is no true believer while he fornicates.'[3]

	Narrator	Compiler(s)
1	Ibn ʿAbbās	Būkhārī (6782) and Muslim
2	Abū Hurayrah	Būkhārī (2475) and Muslim (100)
3	ʿAbdullāh ibn Abī Awfā	Aḥmad (19102)
4	Ibn ʿUmar	Aḥmad[4]

1 Ibn al-Muqri', *Muʿjam* (429).

2 This hadith has also been related from Abū Mālik al-Ashʿarī (Ṭabarānī, *Kabīr*, 3444) and Kaʿb ibn ʿĀṣim al-Ashʿarī (Ṭabarānī, *Kabīr*, 400).

3 This hadith provides a clear indication for the correctness of the belief of the People of the Sunnah (*Ahl as-Sunnah*) that faith consists of conviction in the heart, speech with the tongue and action with the limbs and is subject to increase and decrease. This is contrary to the Murji'ah, who claim that sin does not affect one's faith, and the Khawārij, who claim that the perpetrator of a major sin is a disbeliever. The truth as indicated in the hadith is that the faith of a sinful Muslim is deficient, as the Prophet ﷺ negated perfect faith from him; yet he is not outside the fold of Islam, as the Prophet ﷺ qualified the negation of faith with being in the actual state of committing sin.

4 Bazzār (9435).

5	ʿĀ'ishah	Aḥmad (25088)
6	ʿAlī	Ṭabarānī, *Ṣaghīr* (906)
7	ʿAbdullāh ibn Mughaffal	Ṭabarānī[1]
8	Abū Saʿīd al-Khudrī	Ṭabarānī, *Awsaṭ* (534)
9	Sharīk, on the authority of a man from the Companions	Ṭabarānī, *Kabīr* (7224)

٧ - الْحَيَاءَ مِنْ الإِيمَانِ.

7. 'Modesty is a part of faith.'

	Narrator	*Compiler(s)*
1	Abū Hurayrah	Būkhārī (9) and Muslim (57)
2	Ibn ʿUmar	Būkhārī (24) and Muslim (59)
3	Abū Umāmah	Tirmidhī (2027) and Ḥākim (17)
4	Abū Bakrah	Tirmidhī (2009) and Ḥākim (171)
5	ʿAbdullāh ibn Salām	Abū Yaʿlā, *Musnad* (7501)
6	Ibn ʿAbbās	Ṭabarānī, *Awsaṭ* (8313)[2]
7	Ibn Masʿūd	Ṭabarānī, *Kabīr* (10442)
8	ʿImrān ibn Ḥuṣayn	Ṭabarānī, *Awsaṭ* (8607)
9	Abū Mūsā	Ṭabarānī, *Awsaṭ* (4471)[3]
10	Qurrah ibn Iyās	Ṭabarānī, *Kabīr* (63)[4]

٨ - سُؤالُ جِبْرِيل عَنِ الْإِيْمَانِ وَالْإِسْلَامِ وَالْإِحْسَانِ.

8. The Hadith of Jibrīl.[5]

---

1 Marwazī, *Taʿẓīm Qadr aṣ-Ṣalāh* (555).

2 He has related a different hadith with a similar meaning.

3 Ṭabarāni has quoted a similar hadith from Abū Mūsā.

4 This hadith has also been related from Yazīd ibn Talḥah ibn Rukānah (Ibn Abī Shaybah, 25353).

5 See appendix for a variation of the hadith.

	Narrator	Compiler(s)
1	Abū Hurayrah	Būkhārī (50) and Muslim (9)
2	ʿUmar	Muslim (8)
3	Abū Dharr	Muslim[1]
4	Anas	Būkhārī in *Khalq Afʿāl al-ʿIbād* (p.57)
5	Ibn ʿAbbās	Aḥmad (2924)
6	Ibn ʿUmar	Aḥmad (5856)
7	Abū ʿĀmir al-Ashʿarī	Aḥmad (17167)
8	Jarīr al-Bajalī	Abū ʿUwānah[2]

٩ - الْإِيْمَانُ يَمَانٍ.

9. 'Faith is Yemeni.'[3]

	Narrator	Compiler(s)
1	Abū Hurayrah	Būkhārī (3499) and Muslim (82)
2	Anas	Aḥmad (13346)
3	ʿAmr ibn ʿAnbasah	Aḥmad (19446)
4	ʿUthmān	Ibn as-Sunnī[4]
5	Ibn ʿUmar[5]	Ṭabarānī, *Kabīr* (96)
6	Ibn Masʿūd	Ṭabarānī, *Kabīr* (10055)
7	ʿUqbah ibn ʿĀmir[6]	Ṭabarānī, *Kabīr* (851)
8	ʿAbdullāh ibn ʿAwf	Ṭabarānī[7]
9	Abū Kabshah al-Anmārī	Ṭabarānī, *Kabīr* (857)
10	Ibn ʿAbbās	Bazzār[8]
11	Rawḥ ibn Zinbāʿ al-Judhāmī	Abū Nuʿaym[9]

1 Nasāʾī (4991)
2 Ājurrī, *Sharīʿah* (380).
3 There will always be people of strong faith in Yemen.
4 Bazzār (410).
5 Ṭabarānī has ʿAbdullāh ibn ʿAmr in the reference above.
6 Ṭabarānī has also quoted this hadith from ʿUqbah ibn ʿAmr in *Kabīr* (577).
7 Ibn Abī Shaybah (32437).
8 Nasāʾī, *As-Sunan al-Kubrā* (11648).
9 Ibn Abī ʿĀṣim, *Āḥād* (2268).

١٠ - أَكْمَلُ الْمُؤْمِنِينَ إِيمَانًا أَحْسَنُهُمْ خُلُقًا.

10. 'The believer with the most complete faith is the one with the best character.'

Ibn ʿUmar said in a version narrated by Bazzār: 'I was with Allah's Messenger ﷺ as the tenth of ten people: Abū Bakr, ʿUmar, ʿUthmān, ʿAlī, Ibn Masʿūd, Ḥudhayfah, Abū Saʿīd al-Khudrī and another man (he named) and myself - when a young man from the Helpers came, greeted us, and sat down. He then said, "O Messenger of Allah, who are the best believers?" He replied, "Those of you with the best character."'

	Narrator	*Compiler(s)*
1	Ibn ʿAmr ibn al-ʿĀṣ	Būkhārī (3559)[1]
2	Abū Hurayrah	Ḥākim (1)
3	ʿĀ'ishah	Ḥākim (173)
4	Ḥasan (with no Companion mentioned in the chain)	Ibn Abī Shaybah (30435)
5	ʿUmayr ibn Qatādah	Ṭabarānī, *Awsaṭ* (8123)
6	Abū Saʿīd al-Khudrī	Ṭabarānī[2]
7	Anas	Abū Yaʿlā, *Musnad* (4166)
8	Jābir ibn ʿAbdillāh	Bazzār[3]
9	Ibn ʿUmar	Bazzār (6175)

1 Bukhārī has related a variation of this hadith with a similar meaning.

2 Bayhaqī in *Shuʿab al-īmān* (7616).

3 Ibn Abī Shaybah (30393).

The Book of Ritual Purity

١١ - سُئِلَ عَنْ الْبَحْرِ فَقَالَ: الطَّهُورُ مَاؤُهُ الحِلُّ مَيْتَتُهُ.

11. The Prophet ﷺ was asked about the ocean and he replied, 'Its water is pure and its dead is permissible to eat.'

	Narrator	*Compiler(s)*
1	Abū Hurayrah	Būkhārī[1]
2	ʿAlī	Ḥākim (499)
3	Jābir ibn ʿAbdillāh	Ḥākim (500)
4	Ibn ʿAbbās	Ḥākim (490)
5	Ibn ʿUmar	Ḥākim[2]
6	Abū Bakr aṣ-Ṣiddīq	Dāraquṭnī (72)
7	Anas	Dāraquṭnī (75)
8	Ibn ʿUmar[3]	Dāraquṭnī (74)
9	ʿAbdullāh al-Mudlijī	Ṭabarānī[4]
10	Firāsī	Bayhaqī[5]
11	Sulaymān ibn Mūsā (NCM)[6]	ʿAbd ar-Razzāq, *Mūṣānnaf* (319)
12	Yaḥyā ibn Abī Kathīr (NCM)	ʿAbd ar-Razzāq, *Mūṣānnaf* (8656)

1 Mālik (21).

2 Qāsim ibn Sallām, *Ṭuhūr* (248).

3 Dāraquṭnī has quoted it from Ibn ʿAmr in the reference above.

4 Ājurrī, *Sharīʿah* (4033).

5 Bayhaqī quotes this hadith where Abū Hind al-Firāsī relates from Abū Hurayrah (*As-Sunan al-Kubrā*, 3) and Ibn Mājah quotes the hadith where Ibn al-Firāsī relates from the Prophet ﷺ (387).

6 NCM means "with no Companion mentioned" throughout the text.

١٢ - لَا يَقْبَلُ اللهُ صَلَاةً بِغَيْرِ طُهُورٍ وَلَا صَدَقَةً مِنْ غُلُولٍ.

12. 'Allah does not accept the prayer of a person who is not ritually pure, or zakat that is paid from stolen spoils.'

	Narrator	*Compiler(s)*
1	Ibn ʿUmar	Muslim (224)
2	Usāmah ibn ʿUmayr [father of Abu 'l-Malīḥ]	Abū Dāwūd (59) and Nasā'ī (139)
3	Anas	Ibn Mājah (273)
4	Abū Bakr[1]	Ibn Mājah (274)
5	Zubayr ibn al-ʿAwwām	Ṭabarānī, *Awsaṭ* (6155)
6	Ibn Masʿūd	Ṭabarānī, *Kabīr* (10205)
7	ʿUmar ibn Ḥuṣayn	Ṭabarānī, *Kabīr* (509)
8	Abū Saʿīd al-Khudrī	Ṭabarānī, *Musnad ash-Shāmiyyīn* (2105)
9	Abū Hurayrah	Bazzār (8118)
10	Ḥasan ibn ʿAlī ibn Abī Ṭālib	Khaṭīb, *Al-Muttafaq wa 'l-Muftaraq* (370)[2]

١٣ - المَسْحُ عَلَى الخُفَّيْنِ.

13. Wiping over leather socks. [3]

Ḥasan al-Baṣrī ﵀ said, 'Seventy of the Companions of Allah's Messenger ﷺ told me that he used to wipe over leather socks.' Imam Karkhī ﵀ said, 'I fear disbelief for one who does not consider the wiping over the socks as permissible as it has reached the status of mass transmission.'

1 Ibn Mājah has quoted it from Abū Bakrah.

2 This hadith has also been quoted by Ṭabarānī in *Kabīr* as related from ʿImrān ibn Ḥuṣayn (509).

3 See appendix for a variation of the hadith.

	Narrator	*Compiler(s)*
1	Mughīrah ibn Shuʿbah	Būkhārī (182) and Muslim (274)
2	ʿUmar ibn al-Khaṭṭāb	Būkhārī (202) and Muslim
3	ʿAlī	Būkhārī and Muslim (276)
4	Saʿd ibn Abī Waqqāṣ	Būkhārī)202) and Muslim
5	Bilāl	Būkhārī and Muslim (275)
6	Buraydah	Būkhārī and Muslim (277)
7	Jarīr al-Bajalī	Būkhārī (387) and Muslim (272)
8	Ḥudhayfah	Būkhārī and Muslim (273)
9	ʿAmr ibn Umayyah aḍ-Ḍamrī	Būkhārī (204) and Muslim
10	ʿUbay ibn ʿImārah	Abū Dāwūd (158)
11	Aws ibn Abī Aws	Abū Dāwūd[1]
12	Khuzaymah ibn Thābit	Abū Dāwūd (157)
13	Ṣafwān ibn ʿAsāl	Tirmidhī (96)
14	Jābir ibn ʿAbdillāh	Tirmidhī (94)
15	Abū Bakrah	Ibn Ḥibbān (132) and Ibn Khuzaymah (192)
16	Anas	Ibn Mājah (548)
17	Sahl ibn Saʿd as-Sāʿidī	Ibn Mājah (547)
18	ʿAwf ibn Mālik al-Ashjaʿī	Dāraquṭnī (764)
19	ʿĀʾishah	Dāraquṭnī (2670)
20	Maymūnah	Dāraquṭnī (768)
21	Thawbān	Aḥmad (22419)
22	Abū Ayyūb al-Anṣārī	Aḥmad (23574)
23	Abū Hurayrah	Aḥmad (8695)
24	Usāmah ibn Zayd	Ṭabarānī, *Kabīr* (397)
25	Usāmah ibn Sharīk	Ṭabarānī, *Kabīr* (492)
26	Barāʾ	Ṭabarānī, *Awsaṭ* (5788)
27	Jābir ibn Samurah	Ṭabarānī, *Awsaṭ* (1135)
28	Rabīʿah ibn Kaʿb al-Aslamī	Ṭabarānī, *Kabīr* (4579)
29	Sharīd	Ṭabarānī, *Kabīr* (7248)

1 Aḥmad (16165).

30	ʿUbādah ibn aṣ-Ṣāmit	Ṭabarānī[1]
31	ʿAbdullāh ibn Rawāḥah	Ṭabarānī, *Kabīr* (427)
32	Ibn ʿAbbās	Ṭabarānī, *Awsaṭ* (2931)
33	Ibn ʿUmar	Ṭabarānī, *Awsaṭ* (1566)
34	Ibn Masʿūd	Ṭabarānī, *Kabīr* (924)
35	ʿAbd ar-Raḥmān ibn Ḥasanah	Ṭabarānī[2]
36	ʿIṣmah	Ṭabarānī, *Kabīr* (472)
37	ʿAmr ibn Ḥazm	Ṭabarānī[3]
38	Muslim (father of ʿAwsajah)	Ṭabarānī, *Kabīr* (1057)
39	Maʿqil ibn Yasār	Ṭabarānī, *Kabīr* (507)
40	Yaʿlā ibn Murrah	Ṭabarānī, *Kabīr* (492)
41	Abū Umāmah al-Bāhilī	Ṭabarānī, *Awsaṭ* (1099)
42	Abū Barzah al-Aslamī	Ṭabarānī[4]
43	Abū Saʿīd al-Khudrī	Ṭabarānī, *Awsaṭ* (1037)
44	Abū Ṭalḥah	Ṭabarānī, *Ṣaghīr* (1031)
45	Shayb ibn Ghālib	Ibn Mandah, *Maʿrifat aṣ-Ṣaḥābah*[5]
46	Zayd ibn Ḥazm	Abū Nuʿaym, *Maʿrifah*
47	Ḍaḥḥāk (NCM)	Saʿīd ibn Manṣūr[6]

١٤ - لَا وُضُوءَ لِمَنْ لَمْ يَذْكُرِ اسْمَ اللهِ عَلَيْهِ.

14. 'There is no ablution for whoever does not mention the Name of Allah.'[7]

	Narrator	*Compiler(s)*
1	Saʿīd ibn Zayd	Ḥākim (6899)

1 Ibn Kathīr, *Jāmiʿ al-Masānīd* (5722).

2 Haythamī, *Majmaʿ* (1373).

3 Ibn Abī Usāmah, *Musnad al-Ḥārith* (80).

4 Bazzār (3855).

5 Ibn Kathīr, *Jāmiʿ al-Masānīd* (5097).

6 Bayhaqī, *As-Sunan al-Kubrā* (760).

7 The majority of jurists are of the opinion that saying the *basmallah* is recommended before ablution. With that said, the negation here is understood to be in reference to the complete spiritual benefit of ablution, not its legal validity.

2	Abū Saʿīd	Ḥākim (520)
3	Abū Hurayrah	Ḥākim (518)
4	Abū Sabrah	Ṭabarānī, *Awsaṭ* (1115)
5	Sahl ibn Saʿd	Aḥmad[1]
6	ʿĀ'ishah	Bazzār (307)[2]
7	ʿAlī	Ibn ʿAdī[3]
8	Umm Sabrah	Abū Mūsā, *Maʿrifat aṣ-Ṣahābah*[4]
9	ʿAbd al-Mālik	Abū Mūsā, *Maʿrifat aṣ-Ṣahābah*[5]
10	Anas	Ibn Habīb al-Andalusī[6]

١٥ - أَنَّه صَلَّى اللهُ عَلَيْهِ وَسَلَّمَ كَانَ يُخَلِّلُ لِحْيَتَهُ.

15. Allah's Messenger ﷺ used to comb his beard with his fingers when he washed his face to perform ablution.

	Narrator	*Compiler(s)*
1	Anas	Abū Dāwūd (145)
2	ʿUthmān	Tirmidhī (31)
3	ʿAlī	Tirmidhī[7]
4	Ammār	Tirmidhī (29)
5	Abū Ayyūb	Ibn Mājah (433)
6	ʿĀ'ishah	Aḥmad (25970) and Ḥākim (531)
7	Ibn Abī Awfā	Ṭabarānī, *Awsaṭ* (5332)
8	Ibn ʿAbbās	Ṭabarānī, *Awsaṭ* (2277)
9	Ibn ʿUmar	Ṭabarānī, *Awsaṭ* (1363)
10	Abū Umāmah	Ṭabarānī, *Kabīr* (8070)

1 Ibn Mājah (400).

2 Bazzār quotes a hadith about the Prophet ﷺ starting ablution with the Name of Allah but it is not this same hadith.

3 Ibn Ḥajar, *Talkhīṣ* (1:256).

4 Ibn al-Mulaqqin, *Al-Badr al-Munīr* (2:89).

5 Ibn Ḥajar, *Talkhīs,* (1 p.28).

6 ʿAbd al-Mālik ibn Ḥabīb al-Andalusī has related this with a chain to Anas (Ibn Ḥajar, *Talkhīs,* 1:28). It is possible that narrators 9 and 10 are from the same chain.

7 Bayhaqī in *As-Sunan al-Kubrā* (248).

11	Abu ad-Dardā'	Ṭabarānī[1]
12	Umm Salamah	Ṭabarānī, *Kabīr* (664)
13	Jābir	Ibn ʿAdī (218)
14	Jarīr	Ibn ʿAdī[2]
15	Jubayr ibn Nufayr (NCM)	Saʿīd ibn Manṣūr, *Sunan*[3]

١٦ - وَيْلٌ لِلْأَعْقَابِ مِنَ النَّارِ.

16. 'Woe to the heels being burned in the Fire!'[4]

	Narrator	*Compiler(s)*
1	Ibn ʿUmar[5]	Būkhārī (60) and Muslim (241)
2	Abū Hurayrah	Būkhārī (165) and Muslim (242)
3	ʿĀ'ishah	Muslim (240)
4	Jābir ibn ʿAbdillāh	Ibn Mājah (454), Ibn Abī Shaybah (268) and Saʿīd ibn Manṣūr
5	ʿAbdullāh ibn al-Ḥārith ibn Jaz' (Zubaydī)	Ḥākim (580)
6	Muʿayqīb	Aḥmad (15510)
7	Abū Umāmah	Ṭabarānī, *Kabīr* (8110)
8	Abū Umāmah's brother	Ṭabarānī, *Kabīr* (8109)
9	Abū Dharr	ʿAbd ar-Razzāq, *Mūṣānnaf* (64) and Saʿīd ibn Manṣūr

١٧ - مَنْ مَسَّ فَرْجَهُ فَلْيَتَوَضَّأْ.

17. 'Whoever touches his private parts must perform ablution.'[6]

---

1 Haythamī, *Majmaʿ* (1205).

2 Ibn Ḥajar, *Talkhīṣ* (1:277).

3 Ibn Ḥajar, *Talkhīṣ* (87).

4 By failing to wash them properly in ablution.

5 Bukhārī and Muslim have listed the narrator as Ibn ʿAmr.

6 This is the relied-upon opinion in the Mālikī, Shāfiʿī and Ḥanbalī schools. The Ḥanafīs are of the opinion that touching the private part does not nullify ablution, based

	Narrator	*Compiler(s)*
1	Busrah bint Ṣafwān	Tirmidhī (82), Nasā'ī (163), Ibn Mājah (479) and Abū Dāwūd (181)
2	Ṭalq ibn ʿAlī[1]	Tirmidhī (85), Nasā'ī (165), Ibn Mājah (182) and Abū Dāwūd (182)
3	Jābir	Ibn Mājah (480)
4	Umm Ḥabībah	Ibn Mājah (481)
5	Saʿd ibn Abī Waqqāṣ	Ḥākim (479)
6	Abū Hurayrah	Ḥākim (479)
7	Umm Salamah	Ḥākim (479)
8	Zayd ibn Khālid al-Juhanī	Aḥmad (21689)
9	Ibn ʿAmr	Aḥmad (7076)
10	Ibn ʿUmar	Bazzār (5962)
11	ʿĀ'ishah	Bazzār (131)
12	Ibn ʿAbbās	Bayhaqī, *As-Sunan aṣ-Ṣaghīr* (33)
13	Arwā bint Unays	Bayhaqī[2]
14	Ubayy ibn Kaʿb	Ibn Mandah[3]
15	Anas	Ibn Mandah[4]
16	Qabīṣah	Ibn Mandah[5]
17	Muʿāwiyah ibn Ḥaydah	Ibn Mandah[6]
18	Nuʿmān ibn Bashīr	Ibn Mandah[7]

on the hadith on the authority of Qays ibn Ṭalq from his father: 'We came to the Prophet ﷺ and a man who appeared like a Bedouin came and said: "O Prophet of Allah! What do you think of a man touching his private part after he has performed ablution?" He ﷺ said: "Is it anything but a piece of him?"' (Ibn Mājah (483), Abū Dāwūd (182), Tirmidhī (85) and Nasā'ī (165).)

1 Suyūṭī has listed Ṭalq as a narrator for this hadith but his narration states that there is no ablution from touching private parts.

2 Tirmidhī lists Arwā among other narrators who have related this hadith.

3 Ibn Ḥajar, *Talkhīṣ* (1:346).

4 Ibid.

5 Ibid.

6 Ibn Ḥajar, *Talkhīṣ* (1:342).

7 Ibn Ḥajar, *Talkhīṣ* (1:346).

١٨ - تَوَضَّئُوا مِمَّا مَسَّتِ النَّارُ.

18. 'Perform ablution from whatever fire touches.'[1]

	Narrator	*Compiler(s)*
1	Zayd ibn Thābit	Muslim (351)
2	Abū Hurayrah	Muslim (352)
3	ʿĀ'ishah	Muslim (353)
4	Abū Ayyūb al-Anṣārī	Nasā'ī, *As-Sunan al-Kubrā* (181)
5	Abū Ṭalḥah	Nasā', *As-Sunan al-Kubrā* (180)
6	Anas	Ibn Mājah (487)
7	Sahl ibn al-Ḥanẓaliyyah	Aḥmad (17623)

1 Nawawi ﷺ states in his commentary on *Ṣaḥīḥ Muslim*:

Muslim ﷺ mentions in this chapter the hadiths related about ablution from whatever fire touches. Then he follows them up with hadiths related about leaving ablution from whatever fire touches. It is as if he is pointing to the abrogation of ablution, and this is the norm of Imam Muslim and others: they mention the hadiths that they narrate that are abrogated, then follow them up with the abrogating. The scholars have disagreed about his ﷺ statement: 'Perform ablution from whatever fire touches.' The overwhelming majority of the scholars from the earlier generations and the later generations are of the opinion that eating what fire has touched does not nullify ablution. Among those who were of that opinion are Abū Bakr aṣ-Ṣiddīq, ʿUmar ibn al-Khaṭṭāb, ʿUthman ibn ʿAffān, ʿAlī ibn Abi Ṭālib, ʿAbdullāh ibn Masʿūd, Abu ad-Dardā', Ibn ʿAbbās, ʿAbdullāh ibn ʿUmar, Anas ibn Mālik, Jābir ibn Samurah, Zayd ibn Thābit, Abū Mūsā, Abū Hurayrah, Ubay ibn Kaʿb, Abū Ṭalḥah, ʿĀmir ibn Rabīʿah, Abū Umāmah and ʿĀ'ishah ﷺ. All of these are Companions. The overwhelming majority of the Successors were of that opinion; and it is the opinion of Mālik, Abū Ḥanīfah, Shāfiʿī, Aḥmad, Isḥāq ibn Rahawayh, Yaḥyā ibn Yaḥyā and Abū Khaythamah ﷺ. A group is of the opinion that the legislated ablution (the ablution of the prayer) is obligatory with the eating of whatever fire touches. This is related from ʿUmar ibn ʿAbd al-ʿAzīz, Ḥasan al-Baṣrī, Zuhrī, Qilābah and Abū Majlaz. These adduced the hadith, 'Perform ablution from whatever fire touches.' The overwhelming majority adduced the hadiths relating leaving ablution from what fire touches. There are two responses to the hadith on ablution from whatever fire touches:

The first of them is that it is abrogated by the hadith of Jābir ﷺ. He said, 'The last of the two matters from Allah's Messenger ﷺ was leaving ablution from what fire touched.' It is a sound hadith narrated by Abū Dāwūd, Nasā'ī and others from the people of *Sunan* with sound chains.

The second response is that the meaning of ablution is washing the mouth and the hands. Furthermore, the disagreement we have spoken of was in the first generations; thereafter, the scholars unanimously agreed that ablution with eating whatever fire touched is not obligatory, and Allah knows best.

8	Abū Mūsā	Aḥmad (19552)
9	Umm Salamah	Aḥmad (26724)
10	Ibn ʿUmar	Ṭabarānī, *Awsaṭ* (1914)
11	ʿAbdullāh ibn az-Zubayr	Ṭabarānī[1]
12	Abū Saʿd al-Khayr	Ṭabarānī, Kabīr (776)
13	Muʿādh	Bazzār[2]
14	Umm Ḥabībah	Ḥārith, *Musnad*, and Ibn Abī Shaybah, *Muṣannaf* (550)

١٩ - الْمَاءُ مِنْ الْمَاءِ.

19. 'The purifying bath is only from ejaculate.'[3]

	Narrator	*Compiler(s)*
1	Abū Saʿīd	Muslim (343)
2	Ubayy ibn Kaʿb	Aḥmad (21087)
3	Rāfiʿ ibn Khadīj	Aḥmad (17288)
4	Rifāʿah ibn Rāfiʿ	Aḥmad (21096)
5	ʿItbān al-Anṣārī	Aḥmad (19013)
6	Abū Ayyūb	Aḥmad (23531)

1 Ḥākim (6176).

2 Bayhaqī has quoted a narration from Muʿādh where he states the opposite. Muʿādh was asked about it and he replied, 'People have heard it but have not understood it. We used to call the washing of the hands and the mouth *wuḍū'* and it is not necessary. The Messenger of Allah ﷺ merely told the believers that they should wash their hands and mouths from what is cooked.' (*As-Sunan al-Kubrā* (668).)

3 Imām Nawawī says in his commentary on *Ṣaḥīh Muslim*:

In this chapter is the hadith, "The purifying bath is only from ejaculate." It is from the hadith of Ubayy ibn Kaʿb, related from Allah's Messenger ﷺ, regarding a man who sleeps with his wife yet does not climax. He said, "He must wash his private part and perform ablution." There is another hadith that states, "If one of you lays between her four limbs and begins intercourse, then a purifying bath is required of him, even if he does not climax." The scholars have said that this is the hadith to be practised. As for the hadith, "The purifying bath is only from ejaculate," the majority of the Companions and those after them said that it is indeed abrogated. They meant by abrogated that bathing after sex without climaxing was omitted and then made obligatory.

7	ʿAbd ar-Raḥmān ibn ʿAwf	Bazzār[1]
8	Jābir	Bazzār[2]
9	Ibn ʿAbbās	Bazzār[3]
10	Abū Hurayrah	Bazzār[4]
	Anas	Ibn Shāhīn in *An-Nāsikh wa 'l-Mansūkh*[5]

٢٠ - لَوْلَا أَنْ أَشُقَّ عَلَى أُمَّتِي لَأَمَرْتُهُمْ بِالسِّوَاكِ عِنْدَ كُلِّ صَلَاةٍ. وفي لَفْظٍ عِنْدَ كُلِّ وُضُوءٍ.

20. 'Were it not for the possible difficulty I would be placing on my community, I would have commanded them to use the toothstick (*siwāk*) to brush their teeth at every prayer.' And in a variant narration, 'with every ablution.'

	Narrator	*Compiler(s)*
1	Abū Hurayrah	Būkhārī (887) and Muslim (252)
2	Zayd ibn Khālid al-Juhanī	Abū Dāwūd (47), Tirmidhī (23), and Nasā'ī, *As-Sunan al-Kubrā* (3029)
3	Abū Saʿīd	Nasā'ī, *As-Sunan al-Kubrā* (3018)
4	ʿAlī	Aḥmad (607)
5	Tammām ibn al-ʿAbbās	Aḥmad (1835)
6	Tammām's brother, Qutham[6]	Aḥmad (15656)
7	An unnamed Companion	Aḥmad (23486)
8	Zaynab bint Jaḥsh	Aḥmad (27415)
9	Umm Habībah	Aḥmad (26763)

1 Haythamī, *Majmaʿ* (1433).
2 Haythamī, *Majmaʿ* (1436).
3 ʿAbd ar-Razzāq, *Muṣannaf* (967).
4 Ṭaḥāwī, *Sharḥ Maʿānī al-Āthār* (314).
5 Ibn al-Mulaqqin, *Al-Badr al-Munīr* (2:516).
6 Aḥmad records this hadith from Qutham, the son of Tammām, or Tammām, the son of Qutham.

10	Jaʿfar ibn Abī Ṭālib	Ṭabarānī[1]
11	ʿAbbās ibn ʿAbd al-Muṭṭalib	Ṭabarānī[2]
12	Ibn ʿAbbās	Ṭabarānī, *Kabīr* (11125)
13	Ibn ʿUmar	Ṭabarānī, *Awsaṭ* (8448)
14	ʿĀʾishah	Bazzār (152)
15	Anas	Abū Nuʿaym, *Siwāk*[3]
16	Jābir	Abū Nuʿaym, *Siwāk*[4]
17	Sahl ibn Saʿd	Abū Nuʿaym, *Siwāk*[5]
18	Ibn ʿUmar	Abū Nuʿaym, *Siwāk*[6]
19	Usāmah ibn Zayd	Ibn Manīʿ, *Musnad*
20	Ibn az-Zubayr	Musaddad, *Musnad*[7]
21	ʿAbdullāh ibn Ḥanẓalah	Ibn Mandah, *Musnad*[8]
22	Abū Bakr aṣ-Ṣiddīq	Daylamī[9]
23	Ḥudhayfah	Daylamī[10]
24	Wāthilah	Daylamī[11]
25	Abū Umāmah	Daylamī[12]
26	Abū Ayyūb	Daylamī[13]

1 Abū Yūsuf, *Āthār* (138).

2 Bazzār (1303).

3 Ibn Ḥajar, *Talkhīṣ* (1:226).

4 Ibn Shāhīn, *Targhīb* (511).

5 Ibn al-Mulaqqin, *Al-Badr al-Munīr* (1:701).

6 Tirmidhī includes Ibn ʿUmar in the list of Companions who have related this hadith (167).

7 Ibn Abī Shaybah (1795).

8 Tirmidhī has listed ʿAbdullāh ibn Ḥanẓalah among the narrators who relate this hadith (22). Ibn Ḥanẓalah has also related a hadith about the obligation of using the toothstick for the Prophet ﷺ as is quoted by Aḥmad (2196).

9 Tirmidhī has listed Abū Bakr among the narrators who relate this hadith (22). Aḥmad has recorded a different hadith from Abū Bakr about the toothstick being cleanliness for the mouth and pleasing to the Lord (7).

10 Tirmidhī has listed Ḥudhayfah among the narrators who relate this hadith (22). Bukhārī has recorded a different hadith from Ḥudhayfah about the Prophet ﷺ using the toothstick before the night vigil prayer (245).

11 Wāthilah relates that the Prophet ﷺ said, 'I was commanded to use the toothstick so much that I feared it would be made incumbent on me.' Aḥmad (16007)

12 Tirmidhī has listed Abū Umāmah among the narrators who relate this hadith (22). Ibn Mājah has quoted a similar hadith (289).

13 Tirmidhī has listed Abū Ayyūb among the narrators who relate this hadith (22).

27	Abū Mūsā	Daylamī[1]
28	Umm Salamah	Daylamī[2]

1 Tirmidhī has listed Abū Mūsā among the narrators who relate this hadith (22).

2 Tirmidhī has listed Umm Salamah among the narrators who relate this hadith (22). Ṭabarānī has recorded the hadith of Umm Salamah in which the Prophet ﷺ said, 'Jibrīl persisted in advising me to use the toothstick until I feared for my gums.' *Kabīr* (510).

The Book of Prayer (Ṣalāh)

٢١ - الْمُؤَذِّنُونَ أَطْوَلُ النَّاسِ أَعْنَاقًا يَوْمَ الْقِيَامَةِ.

21. 'Those who make the call to prayer will have the longest necks of all people on the Day of Resurrection.'[1]

	Narrator	*Compiler(s)*
1	Muʿāwiyah ibn Abī Sufyān	Muslim (387)
2	Anas	Aḥmad (12729)
3	Bilāl	Ṭabarānī, *Kabīr* (1080)
4	Zayd ibn Arqam	Ṭabarānī, *Awsaṭ* (2851)
5	Ibn az-Zubayr	Ṭabarānī, *Awsaṭ* (6309)
6	ʿUqbah ibn ʿĀmir	Ṭabarānī, *Kabīr* (777)
7	Abū Hurayrah	Ṭabarānī, *Awsaṭ* (6851)
8	Ibn ʿUmar	Ṭabarānī[2]
9	ʿĪsā, on the authority of an unnamed man from the Companions	ʿAbd ar-Razzāq, *Muṣannaf* (1862)

٢٢ - يُغْفَرُ لِلْمُؤَذِّنِ مَدَى صَوْتِهِ.

22. 'The one who makes the call to prayer is forgiven to the extent of his voice.'

1 This is a figure of speech indicating prominence and honour.

2 Ṭarsūsī, *Musnad ʿAbdillāh ibn ʿUmar* (13)

	Narrator	Compiler(s)
1	Abū Hurayrah	Abū Dāwūd (515) and Nasā'ī (645)
2	Barā' ibn ʿĀzib	Nasā'ī (646)
3	Abū Saʿīd	Aḥmad (11305)[1]
4	Ibn ʿUmar	Aḥmad (6201)
5	Anas	Ṭabarānī, *Awsaṭ* (1987)
6	Abū Umāmah	Ṭabarānī, *Kabīr* (7942)
7	Jābir	Khaṭīb, *Muwaḍḍiḥ*[2]

٢٣ - إِنَّ جِبْرِيْلَ صَلّى بِالنَّبِي صَلَّى اللهُ عَلَيْهِ وَآلِهِ وَسَلَّمَ.

23. The hadith on the prayer times that begins, 'Jibrīl prayed with the Prophet ﷺ. . . .'[3]

	Narrator	Compiler(s)
1	Ibn ʿAbbās	Abū Dāwūd (393) and Tirmidhī (149)
2	Jābir	Nasā'ī (526) and Ḥākim (704)
3	Abū Hurayrah	Nasā'ī (502) and Ḥākim (696)
4	Anas	Dāraquṭnī (1022)
5	Ibn ʿUmar	Dāraquṭnī (1018)
6	Abū Saʿīd	Aḥmad (11249)
7	ʿAmr ibn Ḥazm	Ibn Rāhawayh, *Musnad*[4]
8	Abū Masʿūd al-Anṣārī	Ibn Rāhawayh, *Musnad*[5]
9	One of ʿUmar's sons (NCM)	Saʿīd ibn Manṣūr

1 Aḥmad relates a similar hadith from Abū Saʿīd which states that every jinn, man and everything else will bear witness on the Day of Judgement on behalf of the one who calls to prayer (11305).

2 Ibn Shāhīn, *Targhīb* (567).

3 See appendix for a variation of the hadith.

4 Zaylaʿī, *Naṣb ar-Rāyah* (1:225).

5 Ṭabarānī, *Awsaṭ* (8694).

٢٤ - إِذَا اشْتَدَّ الْحَرُّ فَأَبْرِدُوا بِالصَّلَاةِ، فَإِنَّ شِدَّةَ الْحَرِّ مِنْ فَيْحِ جَهَنَّمَ.

24. 'If the temperature becomes extremely hot, then delay the prayer until it is cooler; for truly, extreme heat is from the breath of Hell.'

	Narrator	*Compiler(s)*
1	Abū Dharr	Būkhārī (535) and Muslim (616)
2	Abū Hurayrah	Būkhārī (536) and Muslim (615)
3	Ibn ʿUmar	Būkhārī (533)
4	Abū Saʿīd	Būkhārī (538)
5	Abū Mūsā	Nasāʾī (501)
6	Mughīrah ibn Shuʿbah	Ibn Mājah (680) and Ibn Ḥibbān (1505)
7	ʿĀʾishah	Ibn Khuzaymah[1]
8	Ṣafwān (Qāsim's father)	Ḥākim (5092)
9	ʿAbd ar-Raḥmān ibn al-Ḥārith	Ṭabarānī[2]
10	ʿAmr ibn ʿAbasah	Ṭabarānī, *Musnad ash-Shāmiyyīn* (1401)
11	An unnamed man, who [Ṭabarānī] thinks is ʿAbdullāh	Ṭabarānī (9793)
12	ʿUmar ibn al-Khaṭṭāb	Abū Yaʿlā[3]
13	Ibn ʿAbbās	Bazzār[4]
14	ʿAbd ar-Raḥmān ibn ʿAlqamah	Abū Nuʿaym[5]
15	Ibn ʿAbbās	Abū Nuʿaym
16	ʿAṭāʾ ibn Yasār (NCM)	Mālik (12)
17	Ḥajjāj al-Bāhilī (a Companion)	Baghawī, *Muʿjam*[6]

1 Abū Yaʿlā, *Musnad* (4949).

2 Some editions refer to ʿAbd ar-Raḥmān ibn Jāriyah, as is recorded in *Naṣb ar-Rāyah* (1:228).

3 Tirmidhī says that this hadith's attribution to ʿUmar from the Prophet ﷺ is not correct.

4 Ibn Ḥajar, *Talkhīṣ* (261).

5 Ibid.

6 Zaylaʿī, *Naṣb ar-Rāyah* (1:228).

٢٥ - أَسْفِرُوا بِالْفَجْرِ فَهُوَ أَعْظَمُ لِلْأَجْرِ.

25. 'Perform the dawn prayer when the sky turns yellow, for it is greater in reward.'

	Narrator	Compiler(s)
1	Rāfiʿ ibn Khadīj	Tirmidhī (154), Nasā'ī (548), Ibn Mājah (672) and Abū Dāwūd (424)
2	Maḥmūd ibn Labīd	Aḥmad (23635)
3	Bilāl	Ṭabarānī[1]
4	Ibn Masʿūd	Ṭabarānī, *Kabīr* (10381)
5	Abū Hurayrah	Ṭabarānī, *Awsaṭ* (3618)
6	Hawwā'	Ṭabarānī, *Kabīr* (563)
7	Anas	Bazzār (6244)
8	Qatādah	Bazzār[2]
9	A man from the Companions	ʿIrāqī, *Musnad*[3]

٢٦ - نَوْمُهُ صَلَّى اللهُ عَلَيْهِ وَسَلَّمَ عَنْ صَلَاةِ الصُّبْحِ فِي الْوَادِي.

26. The Prophet ﷺ slept past the dawn prayer while in the Valley [of al-Qurā].[4]

	Narrator	Compiler(s)
1	ʿImrān ibn Ḥuṣayn	Būkhārī and Muslim (682)
2	Abū Qatādah	Būkhārī (595) and Muslim (681)
3	Abū Hurayrah	Muslim (680)
4	Dhū Mikhbar	Abū Dāwūd (445)
5	ʿAmr ibn Umayyah aḍ-Ḍamrī	Abū Dāwūd (444)
6	Jubayr ibn Muṭʿim	Nasā'ī (624)
7	Abū Maryam as-Salūlī	Nasā'ī (621)

---

1 Bazzār (1356).

2 Ṭabarānī, *Kabīr* (16).

3 Ṭabarānī has related this hadith in *Kabīr* from a man from the Anṣār (4294).

4 See appendix for a variation of the hadith.
This incident took place on the way back to Madīnah after the Battle of Khaybar.

8	Ibn Masʿūd	Aḥmad (3657)
9	Ibn ʿAbbās	Aḥmad
10	Bilāl	Ṭabarānī, *Kabīr* (1079)
11	Jundub	Ṭabarānī, *Kabīr* (1722)[1]
12	Ibn ʿAmr	Ṭabarānī
13	Abū Umāmah	Ṭabarānī
14	Abū Juḥayfah	Ṭabarānī, *Kabīr* (268)
15	Anas	Bazzār

٢٧ - لَا صَلَاةَ بَعْدَ الصُّبْحِ حَتَّى تَطْلُعَ الشَّمْسُ، لَا صَلَاةَ بَعْدَ الْعَصْرِ حَتَّى تَغْرُبَ الشَّمْسُ.

27. 'There is no prayer after the dawn prayer until after the sun rises, and there is no prayer after the late afternoon prayer until the sun has set.'

	Narrator	*Compiler(s)*
1	Abū Saʿīd	Bukhārī (586) and Muslim (827)
2	Abū Hurayrah	Bukhārī (588) and Muslim (825)
3	ʿUmar	Bukhārī (581) and Muslim (826)
4	Ibn ʿAmr[2]	Bukhārī (585) and Muslim (828)
5	ʿAmr ibn ʿAnbasah	Bukhārī and Muslim
6	ʿUqbah ibn ʿĀmir	Bukhārī and Muslim (831)
7	ʿĀʾishah	Bukhārī and Muslim
8	Muʿāwiyah	Bukhārī (587)
9	Anas	Bazzār (6460)
10	Ibn Masʿūd	Bazzār
11	Zayd ibn Thābit	Aḥmad (21661)
12	Saʿd ibn Abī Waqqaṣ	Aḥmad (1469)

1 The reference for Jundub is a variation where some Companions were travelling with the Prophet ﷺ and they missed their prayer.

2 Bukhārī and Muslim record the hadith from Ibn ʿUmar. Ibn ʿAmr's hadith is recorded by Aḥmad (6681).

13	Samurah	Aḥmad (20169)
14	Kaʿb ibn Murrah (or Murrah ibn Kaʿb)	Aḥmad (18059)
15	Abū Umāmah	Aḥmad (22245)
16	Ṣafwān ibn al-Muʿaṭṭal	[ʿAbdullah] ibn Aḥmad (22661)
17	Abū Dharr	Ṭabarānī (847)

٢٨ - مَنْ بَنَى لِلّٰهِ مَسْجِدًا بَنَى اللهُ لَهُ بَيْتًا فِي الْجَنَّةِ.

28. 'Whoever builds a mosque for Allah's sake, Allah shall build a home for him in Paradise.'

	Narrator	*Compiler(s)*
1	ʿUthmān	Būkhārī (450) and Muslim (533)
2	Anas	Tirmidhī (319)
3	ʿAmr ibn ʿAbasah	Nasā'ī (688)
4	ʿUmar	Ibn Mājah (735)
5	ʿAlī	Ibn Mājah (737)
6	Jābir ibn ʿAbdillāh	Ibn Mājah (738)
7	Ibn ʿAbbās	Aḥmad (2157)
8	Ibn ʿUmar	Aḥmad (7056)[1]
9	Wāthilah ibn al-Asqaʿ	Aḥmad (16005)
10	Asmā' bint Yazīd	Aḥmad (27612)
11	Abū Bakr aṣ-Ṣiddīq	Ṭabarānī, *Awsaṭ* (7114)
12	Ibn ʿUmar	Ṭabarānī, *Awsaṭ* (6167)
13	Nubayṭ ibn Shurayṭ	Ṭabarānī, *Awsaṭ* (2215)
14	Abū Umāmah	Ṭabarānī, *Kabīr* (7889)
15	Abū Dharr	Ṭabarānī, *Ṣaghīr* (1105)
16	Abū Qirṣāfah	Ṭabarānī, *Kabīr* (2521)
17	Abū Hurayrah	Ṭabarānī, *Awsaṭ* (4641)
18	ʿĀ'ishah	Ṭabarānī, *Awsaṭ* (6586)

1 I could not find Ibn ʿUmar but Aḥmad has recorded this hadith from Ibn ʿAmr in the reference given above.

19	ʿAbdullāh ibn Abī Awfā	Rāfiʿī[1]
20	Muʿādh ibn Jabal	Ibn ʿAsākir, *Tārīkh* (3126)
21	Umm Ḥabībah	Ibn ʿAsākir, *Tārīkh* (5439)

٢٩ - بَشِّرِ الْمَشَّائِينَ فِي الظُّلَمِ إِلَى الْمَسَاجِدِ بِالنُّورِ التَّامِّ يَوْمَ الْقِيَامَةِ.

29. 'Give those who walk to the mosque in darkness the good news that consummate light is theirs on the Day of Resurrection!'

	Narrator	*Compiler(s)*
1	Buraydah	Abū Dāwūd (561) and Tirmidhī (223)
2	Anas	Ibn Mājah (781) and Ḥākim (769)
3	Sahl ibn Saʿd	Ibn Mājah (780) and Ḥākim (768)
4	Zayd ibn Ḥārithah	Ṭabarānī, *Awsaṭ* (4581)
5	Ibn ʿAbbās	Ṭabarānī, *Kabīr* (10689)
6	Ibn ʿUmar	Ṭabarānī, *Kabīr* (13335)
7	Abū Umāmah	Ṭabarānī, *Kabīr* (7633)
8	Abu ad-Dardā'	Ṭabarānī, *Awsaṭ* (4697)
9	Abū Hurayrah	Ṭabarānī, *Awsaṭ* (843)
10	ʿĀ'ishah	Ṭabarānī, *Awsaṭ* (1275)
11	Abū Mūsā al-Ashʿarī	Bazzār (3074)
12	Abū Saʿīd al-Khudrī	Ṭayālisī, *Musnad* (2326)
13	Ḥārithah ibn Wahb	Ibn Shāhīn, *Targhīb* (91)
14	Ḥuṭaym ibn al-Ḥaddānī (NCM)	Abū Mūsā al-Madīnī
15	ʿAṭā' ibn Yasār (NCM)	Saʿīd ibn Manṣūr

٣٠ - مَنْ أَكَلَ ثُومًا أَوْ بَصَلًا فَلْيَعْتَزِلْنَا.

30. 'Whoever eats (raw) garlic or onion should keep away from us.'

1 ʿIrāqī, Ibn as-Subkī and Zubaydī, *Takhrīj Aḥādīth Iḥyā'* (389).

	Narrator	*Compiler(s)*
1	Anas	Būkhārī (856) and Muslim (562)
2	Jābir ibn ʿAbdillāh	Būkhārī (854) and Muslim (563)
3	Ibn ʿUmar	Būkhārī (853) and Muslim (561)
4	Abū Hurayrah	Muslim (562)
5	Maʿqil ibn Yasār	Aḥmad (20302)[1]
6	Abū Bakr aṣ-Ṣiddīq	Ṭabarānī, *Awsaṭ* (613)
7	Bashīr al-Aslamī	Ṭabarānī, *Kabīr* (1225)
8	Khuzaymah ibn Thābit	Ṭabarānī
9	ʿAbdullāh ibn Zayd	Ṭabarānī, *Awsaṭ* (8550)
10	Abū Thaʿlabah	Ṭabarānī, *Musnad ash-Shāmiyyīn* (1613)
11	Abū Saʿīd	Ṭabarānī, *Awsaṭ* (8663)
12	Jābir ibn Samurah	Bazzār (4282)

٣١ - مِفْتَاحُ الصَّلَاةِ الطُّهُورُ وَتَحْرِيمُهَا التَّكْبِيرُ وَتَحْلِيلُهَا التَّسْلِيمُ.

31. 'The key to prayer is ritual purity, the *takbīr* [i.e. opening with '*Allāhu Akbar*'] is its sanctum and the *taslīm* [i.e. closing with '*salām*'] is its dissolution.'

	Narrator	*Compiler(s)*
1	ʿAlī	Abū Dāwūd (61) and Tirmidhī (3)
2	Jābir	Tirmidhī (4)
3	Abū Saʿīd	Tirmidhī (3)
4	ʿAbdullāh ibn Zayd	Dāraquṭnī (1360)
5	Ibn ʿAbbās	Ṭabarānī, *Awsaṭ* (9267)
6	Ibn Masʿūd	Ṭabarānī[2]
7	Anas	Ibn ʿAdī[3]

1 In this hadith, Aḥmad records an incident related by Maʿqil in which the Prophet ﷺ forbade certain people from praying with the congregation due to the smell of garlic emitting from them.

2 Bayhaqī, *As-Sunan aṣ-Ṣaghīr* (358).

3 Ibn Muqri', *Muʿjam* (441).

٣٢ - الجَهْر بِالْبَسْمَلَةِ.

32. Reciting the *basmallah* out loud.[1]

	Narrator	*Compiler(s)*
1	Anas	Ḥākim (853)
2	Ibn ʿAbbās	Ḥākim (750)
3	Abū Hurayrah	Ḥākim (850)
4	Umm Salamah	Ḥākim (847)
5	ʿUthmān	Dāraquṭnī[2]
6	ʿAlī	Dāraquṭnī (1155)
7	Jābir ibn ʿAbdillāh	Dāraquṭnī (1176)
8	Ḥakam ibn ʿUmayr	Dāraquṭnī (1185)
9	Ibn ʿUmar	Dāraquṭnī (1164)
10	Ammār ibn Yāsir	Dāraquṭnī (1158)
11	Nuʿmān ibn Bashīr	Dāraquṭnī (1181)
12	ʿĀ'ishah	Dāraquṭnī (1186)
13	Ubay ibn Kaʿb	Bayhaqī
14	Samurah ibn Jundub	Bayhaqī[3]
15	Buraydah	Khaṭīb, *Basmalah* (17)
16	Bishr or Bashīr ibn Muʿāwiyah	Khaṭīb, *Basmalah*
17	Ḥusayn ibn ʿUrfuṭah	Khaṭīb, *Basmalah*
18	Mujālid ibn Thawr	Khaṭīb, *Basmalah*
19	A group of Emigrants	

---

1 See appendix for a variation of the hadith.

The great Shāfiʿī jurist Qāḍī Abu 'l-Ḥasan al-Māwardī states in *Al-Ḥāwī al-Kabīr*: 'Section: If the obligation of reciting the *Fātiḥah* is established, and '*bismillāhi 'r-Raḥmāni 'r-Raḥīm*' is a verse of it, then its ruling in regards to reciting aloud and reciting quietly is the ruling of reciting the *Fātiḥah*—whether one recites it aloud with the *Fātiḥah* in the loud prayer or recites it quietly with the *Fātiḥah* in the quiet prayer.'

Aḥmad ibn Ḥanbal said: 'One recites it quietly in both the loud and quiet prayers.' Isḥāq (ibn Rāhawayh) said: 'One is free to choose between reciting loudly or quietly.'

2 I could not find this hadith from ʿUthmān. Dāraquṭnī (1203) and others, however, have recorded a hadith from Anas wherein he says he prayed behind the Prophet ﷺ, Abū Bakr, ʿUmar and ʿUthmān and they did not recite the *basmalah* aloud.

3 Khaṭīb, *Basmalah* (17).

	(*Muhājirūn*) and Helpers (*Anṣār*)	Shāfiʿī

٣٣ - رَفْعُ الْيَدَيْنِ فِي الصَّلَاةِ وَالْإِحْرَامِ وَالرُّكُوعِ وَالْاِعْتِدَالِ.

33. Lifting the hands when opening the prayer, when bowing and when straightening back up.[1]

	Narrator	*Compiler(s)*
1	Ibn ʿUmar	Būkhārī (735) and Muslim (390)
2	Mālik ibn al-Ḥuwayrith	Būkhārī (737) and Muslim (391)
3	Wā'il ibn Ḥujr	Muslim (401)
4	ʿAlī	Tirmidhī (3423), Nasā'ī, Ibn Mājah (864) and Abū Dāwūd (744)
5	Sahl ibn Saʿd	Abū Dāwūd (734)
6	Ibn az-Zubayr	Abū Dāwūd (739)
7	Ibn ʿAbbās	Abū Dāwūd[2]
8	Muḥammad ibn Maslamah	Abū Dāwūd (734)
9	Abū Usayd	Abū Dāwūd (733)
10	Abū Ḥumayd	Abū Dāwūd (730)
11	Abū Qatādah	Abū Dāwūd (730)
12	Abū Hurayrah	Abū Dāwūd (738)
13	Anas	Ibn Mājah (866)
14	Jābir ibn ʿAbdillāh	Ibn Mājah (868)
15	ʿUmayr al-Laythī	Ibn Mājah (861)
16	Ḥakam ibn ʿUmayr	Aḥmad[3]
17	A desert Arab	Aḥmad
18	Abū Bakr aṣ-Ṣiddīq	Bayhaqī, *As-Sunan al-Kubrā* (2519)
19	Barā'	Bayhaqī, *As-Sunan al-Kubrā* (2530)

1 See appendix for a variation of the hadith.

2 Ibn Abī Shaybah (2430).

3 Ṭabarānī, *Kabīr* (3190). This hadith only mentions lifting the hands for the beginning of the prayer.

20	ʿUmar ibn al-Khaṭṭāb	Dāraquṭnī[1]
21	Abū Mūsā al-Ashʿarī	Dāraquṭnī (1124)
22	ʿUqbah ibn ʿĀmir	Ṭabarānī, *Kabīr* (819)
23	Muʿādh ibn Jabal	Ṭabarānī, *Kabīr* (139)

٣٤ - حَدِيْثُ التَّشَهُّد.

34. Reciting the testimony of faith (*tashahhud*).[2]

	Narrator	*Compiler(s)*
1	Ibn Masʿūd	Būkhārī (831) and Muslim (402)
2	Ibn ʿAbbās	Muslim (403)
3	Abū Mūsā al-Ashʿarī	Muslim (404)
4	ʿUmar	Ḥākim (979)
5	Jābir	Ḥākim (983)
6	Ibn ʿUmar	Abū Dāwūd (971)
7	Samurah ibn Jundub	Abū Dāwūd (975)
8	ʿĀʾishah	Bayhaqī, *As-Sunan al-Kubrā* (2833)
9	ʿAlī	Ṭabarānī[3]
10	Ibn az-Zubayr	Ṭabarānī, *Awsaṭ* (3116)
11	Muʿāwiyah ibn Abī Sufyān	Ṭabarānī, *Kabīr* (891)

1 Bukhārī, *Qurrat al-ʿAynayn bi-Rafʿi 'l-Yadayn fi 'ṣ-Ṣalāh* (1).

2 See appendix for a variation of the hadith.

There are three wordings of the *tashahhud* that are narrated. The Ḥanafīs and Ḥanbanlīs prefer the *tashahhud* of Ibn Masʿūd: 'Greetings are for Allah, as well as all prayers and all good things. Peace be upon you, O Prophet, and Allah's mercy and blessings. Peace be upon us and Allah's righteous slaves. I testify that there is no god but Allah, and I testify that Muḥammad is His slave and Messenger.'

The Mālikīs prefer the *tashahhud* of ʿUmar: 'Greetings are for Allah; all pure things are for Allah; all prayers and all good things are for Allah. Peace be upon you, O Prophet, and Allah's mercy and blessings. Peace be upon us and Allah's righteous slaves. I testify that there is no god but Allah, and I testify that Muḥammad is His slave and Messenger.'

The Shāfiʿīs prefer the *tashahhud* of Ibn ʿAbbās: 'Greetings, all blessed things, all prayers and all good things are for Allah. Peace be upon you, O Prophet, and Allah's mercy and blessings. Peace be upon us and Allah's righteous slaves. I testify that there is no god but Allah, and I testify that Muḥammad is Allah's Messenger.'

3 Abū ʿUwānah (2041).

12	Salmān	Ṭabarānī, *Kabīr* (6171)
13	Abū Ḥumayd	Ṭabarānī[1]
14	Abū Bakr aṣ-Ṣiddīq	Ibn Marduwayh, *Tashahhud*[2]
15	Ṭalḥah ibn ʿUbaydillāh	Ibn Marduwayh, *Tashahhud*[3]
16	Anas	Ibn Marduwayh, *Tashahhud*[4]
17	Ḥudhayfah	Ibn Marduwayh, *Tashahhud*
18	Ḥusayn ibn ʿAlī	Ibn Marduwayh, *Tashahhud*
19	Ibn Abī Awfā	Ibn Marduwayh, *Tashahhud*[5]
20	Faḍl ibn ʿAbbās	Ibn Marduwayh, *Tashahhud*[6]
21	Abū Saʿīd	Ibn Marduwayh, *Tashahhud*[7]
22	Abū Hurayrah	Ibn Marduwayh, *Tashahhud*[8]
23	Umm Salamah	Ibn Marduwayh, *Tashahhud*[9]

٣٥ - أَنَّهُم قَالُوا قَدْ عَلِمْنَا كَيْفَ نُسَلِّمُ عَلَيْكَ فَكَيْفَ نُصَلِّي عَلَيْكَ.

35. The Companions asked the Prophet ﷺ, 'We know how to greet you with peace, but how do we invoke blessings upon you?'[10]

	Narrator	*Compiler(s)*
1	Kaʿb ibn ʿUjrah	Bukhārī (6357) and Muslim (406)
2	Abū Ḥumayd as-Sāʿidī	Bukhārī (3369) and Muslim (407)
3	Abū Saʿīd	Bukhārī (6358)
4	Abū Masʿūd al-Anṣārī	Muslim (405)
5	Ṭalḥah ibn ʿUbaydillāh	Nasāʾī (1290)

1 Bayhaqī, *Maʿrifat as-Sunan* (3631). This hadith is about the manner in which the Prophet ﷺ sat for *tashahhud*.

2 Ṭaḥāwī, *Sharḥ Maʿānī* (1573).

3 Ibn Ḥajar, *Talkhīṣ* (1:641).

4 Abū Yaʿlā (2833).

5 Haythamī, *Majmaʿ* (2844).

6 Ibn Ḥajar, *Talkhīṣ* (1:641).

7 Ṭabarānī, *Musnad ash-Shāmiyyīn* (1360).

8 Ibn Ḥajar, *Talkhīṣ* (1:482).

9 Ṭabarānī, *Kabīr* (869).

10 See appendix for a variation of the hadith.

6	Zayd ibn Khārijah	Nasā'ī (7625)
7	Buraydah	Aḥmad (22988)
8	Abū Hurayrah	Bazzār (8154)
9	Sahl ibn Sa'd	Ṭabarānī
10	Ruwayfi' ibn Thābit	Mustaghfirī, *Da'awāt*
11	Jābir	Mustaghfirī, *Da'awāt*
12	Ibn 'Abbās	Mustaghfirī, *Da'awāt*
13	Nu'mān ibn Abī 'Ayyāsh	Mustaghfirī, *Da'awāt*

٣٦ - أَنَّ النَّبِيَّ صَلَّى اللهُ عَلَيْهِ وَسَلَّمَ كَانَ يُسَلِّمُ عَنْ يَمِينِهِ السَّلَامُ عَلَيْكُمْ وَرَحْمَةُ اللهِ حَتَّى يُرَى بَيَاضُ خَدِّهِ الْأَيْمَنِ، وَفِي الْأَيْسَرِ كَذلِك.

36. The Prophet ﷺ closed the prayer by saying, '*As-salāmū 'alaykum wa raḥmatullāh*,' and by turning his head to the right until the whiteness of his cheek was seen, and likewise turning it to the left.

	Narrator	*Compiler(s)*
1	Sa'd ibn Abī Waqqāṣ	Muslim (582)
2	Jābir ibn Samurah	Muslim (431)
3	Wā'il ibn Ḥujr	Abū Dāwūd (933)
4	Ibn Mas'ūd	Nasā'ī (1325)
5	Ammār ibn Yāsir	Ibn Mājah (916)
6	Ḥudhayfah	Ibn Mājah[1]
7	'Adī ibn 'Umayrah al-Ḥaḍramī	Ibn Mājah[2]
8	Sahl ibn Sa'd	Aḥmad (22864)
9	Ṭalq ibn 'Alī	Aḥmad (25)
10	Mughīrah ibn Shu'bah	Ṭabarānī, *Kabīr* (929)
11	Abū Rimthah al-Balwī	Ṭabarānī[3]

1 Ibn Ḥajar, *Talkhīṣ* (1:646).
2 Aḥmad (17726).
3 Ḥākim (996).

12	Wāthilah ibn al-Asqaʿ	Shāfiʿī[1]
13	Barāʾ ibn ʿĀzib	Dāraquṭnī (1350)
14	Yaʿqūb ibn al-Ḥuṣayn	Abū Nuʿaym, *Maʿrifah* (6667)

٣٧ - إِنَّ اللّٰهَ زَادَكُمْ صَلَاةً هِيَ خَيْرٌ لَكُمْ مِنْ حُمْرِ النَّعَمِ، وَهِيَ الْوِتْرُ.

37. 'Allah has indeed legislated an additional prayer that is better for you than red camels! It is the *witr* prayer.'[2]

	Narrator	*Compiler(s)*
1	Khārijah ibn Ḥudhāfah	Abū Dāwūd (1418) and Tirmidhī (452)
2	Abū Baṣrah al-Ghifārī	Aḥmad (23851)
3	Muʿādh ibn Jabal	Aḥmad (22095)
4	Ibn ʿAmr	Aḥmad (6693)
5	Ibn ʿAbbās	Ṭabarānī, *Awsaṭ* (2710)
6	ʿUqbah ibn ʿĀmir al-Juhanī	Ṭabarānī, *Awsaṭ* (7975)
7	ʿAmr ibn al-ʿĀṣ	Ṭabarānī, *Kabīr* (2167)
8	Ibn ʿUmar	Ibn Ḥibbān, *Ḍuʿafāʾ* (81)

٣٨ - مَنْ تَرَكَ الْجُمُعَةَ ثَلَاثاً مِنْ غَيْرِ عُذْرٍ طَبَعَ اللّٰهُ عَلَى قَلْبِهِ.

38. 'Allah will seal the heart of whoever skips three Friday prayers without an excuse.'

---

1 Zaylaʿī, *Naṣb* (1:432)

2 The Mālikīs, Shāfiʿīs, and Ḥanbalīs are of the opinion that the *witr* prayer is emphatically recommended (*sunnah muʾakkadah*), contrary to the Ḥanafīs, who are of the opinion that it is required (*wājib*), a degree lesser than obligation (*farḍ*) according to their classification of legal rulings. Thus, the *witr* prayer should not be left, in deference to Imam Abū Ḥanīfah ﷺ and considering the hadith narrated by Abū Dāwūd on the authority of Buraydah: '*Witr* is a right, so whoever does not pray *witr* is not from us! *Witr* is a right, so whoever does not pray *witr* is not from us! *Witr* is a right, so whoever does not pray *witr* is not from us!'

	Narrator	*Compiler(s)*
1	Abu 'l-Ja'd aḍ-Ḍamrī	Tirmidhī (500), Nasā'ī (1369), Ibn Mājah (1125) and Abū Dāwūd (1052)
2	Jābir	Nasā'ī, *As-Sunan al-Kubrā* (1669)
3	Abū Qatādah	Ḥākim (1081)
4	Usāmah	Ṭabarānī, *Kabīr* (422)
5	Ḥādithah ibn an-Nu'mān	Ṭabarānī, *Kabīr* (3229)
6	Ibn 'Amr[1]	Ṭabarānī, *Awsaṭ* (336)
7	Abū Hurayrah	Ṭabarānī, *Awsaṭ* (2828)
8	Ibn Abī Awfā	Ṭabarānī[2]
9	Abū 'Abs ibn Jabr	Abū Nu'aym, *Ma'rifah* (6930)
10	Ibn 'Abbās	Abū Ya'lā (371)[3]
11	Ibn As'ad ibn Zurārah	Abū Ya'lā[4]
12	Ṣafwān ibn Sulaym (NCM)	Mālik (372)

٣٩ - إِذَا أَتَى أَحَدُكُمُ الْجُمُعَةَ فَلْيَغْتَسِلْ.

39. 'When one of you goes to the Friday prayer, he should bathe beforehand.'

	Narrator	*Compiler(s)*
1	Ibn 'Umar	Būkhārī (877) and Muslim (844)
2	Ibn 'Abbās	Aḥmad (3058)
3	Buraydah	Ṭabarānī, *Awsaṭ* (5623)
4	'Ā'ishah	Ṭabarānī, *Awsaṭ* (2127)
5	Abū Ayyūb	Bazzār[5]
6	'Abdullāh ibn az-Zubayr	Bazzār[6]

1 Ṭabaranī relates this hadith from Ibn 'Umar.

2 Haythamī, *Majma'* (3179).

3 Haythamī has recorded a variation of it in *Al-Maqṣad al-'Alī fī Zawā'id Abī Ya'lā al-Mūṣilī*. Ibn Abī Shaybah has also related this hadith (5536).

4 Ibn Abī 'Āṣim, *Āḥād* (2197).

5 Ṭabarānī, *Kabīr* (3971).

6 Ṭabarānī, *Kabīr* (244).

Abu 'l-Qāsim [i.e. Ibn Mandah] says, 'Three-hundred people narrated this hadith on the authority of Nāfiʿ on his [i.e. Ibn ʿUmar's] authority.' Ḥāfiẓ Ibn Ḥajar says, 'I have come across 120 of them.'

As for the general bathing on Friday without specifying, the following have narrated it:

	Narrator	*Compiler(s)*
1	Ibn ʿUmar[1]	Abū Dāwūd (347)
2	Abū Saʿīd	Abū Dāwūd (341)
3	Aws ibn Aws	Abū Dāwūd (345)
4	Abū ad-Dardā'	Aḥmad (21729)
5	Nubayshah al-Hudhalī	Aḥmad (20721)
6	Thawbān	Bazzār (4171)
7	Ibn Masʿūd	Bazzār (1932)
8	Anas	Bazzār (6669)
9	Abū Hurayrah	Ṭabarānī, *Awsaṭ* (2632)
10	Jābir ibn ʿAbdillāh	Ṭabarānī, *Awsaṭ* (4267)
11	Sahl ibn Ḥunayf	Ṭabarānī, *Kabīr* (5596)
12	Abū Umāmah	Ṭabarānī, *Kabīr* (7689)
13	Abū Bakr aṣ-Ṣiddīq	Ṭabarānī, *Awsaṭ* (3397)
14	ʿImrān ibn Ḥuṣayn	Ṭabarānī, *Awsaṭ* (4413)
15	Abū Qatādah	Ṭabarānī, *Awsaṭ* (8180)
16	ʿAbd ar-Raḥmān ibn Samurah	Ṭabarānī, *Awsaṭ* (7765)
17	ʿAlī	Ṭabarānī, *Awsaṭ* (2193)

٤٠ - أَنَّه صَلَّى اللهُ عَلَيْهِ وَسَلَّمَ كَانَ يَذْهَبُ فِي الْعِيدِ فِي طَرِيقٍ وَيَرْجِعُ فِي آخَرَ.

40. The Prophet ﷺ used to go to the Eid prayer on one road and return home on another road.

1 Abū Dāwūd has recorded it as Ibn ʿAmr.

	Narrator	*Compiler(s)*
1	Jābir	Būkhārī (986) and Muslim
2	Ibn ʿUmar	Abū Dāwūd (1156)
3	Abū Hurayrah	Tirmidhī (541) and Ḥākim
4	Saʿd al-Qaraẓ	Ibn Mājah (1298)
5	Abū Rāfiʿ	Ibn Mājah (1300)
6	Saʿīd ibn al-Ḥārith[1]	Bazzār (1115)
7	ʿAbd al-Raḥmān ibn Ḥāṭib	Abū Nuʿaym, *Maʿrifah* (4614)

٤١ - لَقِّنُوا مَوْتَاكُمْ لَا إِلَهَ إِلَّا اللهُ.

41. 'Prompt those of you who are dying to say, "There is no god except Allah."'

	Narrator	*Compiler(s)*
1	Abū Saʿīd	Muslim (916)
2	Abū Hurayrah	Muslim (917)
3	ʿAbdullāh Ibn Jaʿfar	Nasāʾī[2]
4	ʿĀʾishah	Nasāʾī (1827)
5	Ibn ʿAbbās	Ṭabarānī, *Duʿāʾ* (1141)
6	Ibn Masʿūd	Ṭabarānī, *Kabīr* (10417)
7	Jābir ibn ʿAbdillāh	Bazzār[3]
8	ʿUrwah ibn Masʿūd	ʿUqaylī, *Ḍuʿafā*[4]
9	Ḥudhayfah	Ibn Abī ad-Dunyā, *Muḥtaḍarīn* (2)
10	ʿUmar	Ibn Abī ad-Dunyā, *Muḥtaḍarīn* (8)
11	ʿUthmān	Ibn Abī ad-Dunyā, *Muḥtaḍarīn* (5)
12	Anas	Ibn Abī ad-Dunyā, *Muḥtaḍarīn* (11)

1 Bazzār relates this hadith from ʿĀmir, who relates from his father Saʿd in the reference above. Ibn ʿAsākir has mentioned ʿĀmir ibn Saʿd ibn al-Ḥārith in *Tārīkh Dimashq* (3044).

2 Ibn Mājah (1446).

3 Ṭabarānī, *Duʿā* (1141).

4 Abū Nuʿaym, *Maʿrifah* (5488).

٤٢ - أَنَّه صَلَّى اللهُ عَلَيْهِ وَسَلَّمَ مَرَّ بِقَبْرٍ دُفِنَ لَيْلًا، فَقَالَ: مَتَى دُفِنَ، قَالُوا: الْبَارِحَةَ، قَالَ: أَفَلَا آذَنْتُمُونِي. قَالُوا: كَرِهْنَا أَنْ نُوقِظَكَ، فَصَلَّى عَلَيْهِ.

42. The Prophet ﷺ passed by a grave that had been dug the night before, so he asked, 'When was this dug?' The Companions replied, 'Last night.' He said, 'Why did you not let me know?' They said, 'We disliked the thought of waking you up.' He then prayed over it.

	Narrator	*Compiler(s)*
1	Ibn ʿAbbās	Būkhārī (1321) and Muslim (954)
2	Abū Hurayrah	Būkhārī (458) and Muslim (956)
3	ʿUqbah ibn ʿĀmir	Būkhārī[1]
4	Zayd ibn Thābit	Nasāʾī (2022)
5	ʿAbdullāh ibn ʿĀrim ibn Rabīʿah[2]	Nasāʾī[3]
6	Abū Saʿīd	Ibn Mājah (1533)
7	Ibn ʿUmar	Ṭabarānī[4]
8	ʿImrān ibn Ḥuṣayn	Ṭabarānī[5]
9	ʿAmr ibn ʿAwf	Ṭabarānī[6]
10	Anas ibn Mālik	Bazzār[7]
11	Abū Umāmah ibn Sahl	Mālik (772)
12	Buraydah	Ḥarb al-Kirmānī[8]
13	ʿĀmir ibn Rabīʿah	Ḥarb al-Kirmānī[9]
14	ʿUbādah	Ḥarb al-Kirmānī[10]
15	Abū Qatādah	Ḥarb al-Kirmānī [11]

1 Ibn Ḥajar, *Talkhīṣ* (774).

2 This is an error in the transcription. The Companion is ʿAbdullāh ibn ʿĀmir in Rabīʿah.

3 Ibn Mājah (1529).

4 Ibn Ḥajar, *Talkhīṣ* (774).

5 Ibid.

6 Ibid.

7 Ibid.

8 Ibid.

9 Ibid.

10 Ibid.

11 Ibid.

٤٣ - مُرَّ بِجَنَازَةٍ فَأُثْنِيَ عَلَيْهَا خَيْرًا فَقَالَ عَلَيهِ الصَّلاةُ والسَّلَامُ: وَجَبَتْ، ثُمَّ مُرَّ بِأُخْرى فَأُثْنِيَ عَلَيْهَا بِشَرٍّ فَقَالَ: وَجَبَتْ، أَنْتُمْ شُهَدَاءُ اللهِ فِي الْأَرْضِ.

43. The Prophet ﷺ passed by a funeral procession and the deceased was being extolled, so he said: 'It is inevitable.' Thereafter he passed by another funeral procession and the deceased was being spoken ill of, so he said: 'It is inevitable. You are Allah's witnesses on the Earth.

	Narrator	*Compiler(s)*
1	Anas	Būkhārī (1367) and Muslim (949)
2	ʿUmar	Būkhārī (1368)
3	Abū Hurayrah	Aḥmad (7552)
4	Qatādah	Aḥmad[1]
5	Abū Zuhayr	Aḥmad (64)
6	Salamah ibn al-Akwaʿ	Ṭabarānī, *Kabīr* (6259)
7	Kaʿb ibn ʿUjrah	Ṭabarānī, *Kabīr* (344)
8	ʿĀmir ibn Rabīʿah	Bazzār[2]
9	Ibn ʿUmar	Ibn ʿAdī

٤٤ - إِنَّ الْمَيِّتَ يُعَذَّبُ بِبُكَاءِ الْحَيِّ عَلَيْهِ.

44. 'The deceased is indeed punished for the living's wailing over him.'[3]

	Narrator	*Compiler(s)*
1	ʿUmar	Būkhārī (1286) and Muslim (927)
2	Ibn ʿUmar	Būkhārī (1287) and Muslim (929)
3	Ḥafṣah	Muslim (927)
4	Anas	Ibn Ḥibbān (3132)

1 Ibn Ḥajar, *Anīs as-Sārī* (5204).

2 Haythamī, *Majmaʿ* (3965).

3 This applies when he instructs them to do so or fails to disuade them from doing so if it was their habit and custom and he feared this occurring.

5	ʿImrān ibn Ḥuṣayn	Ibn Ḥibbān (3134)
6	Abū Mūsā	Tirmidhī (1003) and Ibn Mājah (1594)
7	Abū Bakr	Abū Yaʿlā (47)
8	Abū Hurayrah	Abū Yaʿlā (1592)[1]
9	Samurah	Ṭabarānī, *Kabīr* (6896)

٤٥ - كُنْتُ نَهَيْتُكُمْ عَنْ زِيَارَةِ الْقُبُورِ فَزُورُوهَا.

45. 'I once forbade you from visiting graves, but now I say visit them.'

	Narrator	*Compiler(s)*
1	Buraydah	Muslim (977)
2	Abū Saʿīd al-Khudrī	Aḥmad (11329)
3	ʿAlī	Aḥmad (1236)
4	Umm Salmah	Ṭabarānī, *Kabīr* (602)
5	Zayd ibn al-Khaṭṭāb	Ṭabarānī, *Kabīr* (4648)
6	Ibn ʿAbbās	Ṭabarānī, *Awsaṭ* (2709)
7	Thawbān	Ṭabarānī, *Kabīr* (1419)
8	ʿĀʾishah	Bazzār (230)

1 This hadith reported by Abū Yaʿlā discusses the difference of opinion the Companions had regarding this issue.

The Book of Zakat

٤٦ - لَا زَكَاةَ فِي مَالٍ حَتَّى يَحُولَ عَلَيْهِ الْحَوْلُ.

46. 'There is no zakat due on wealth until a [lunar] year has passed on it.'

	Narrator	*Compiler(s)*
1	ʿAlī	Abū Dāwūd (1573)
2	ʿĀ'ishah	Ibn Mājah (1792)
3	Anas	Dāraquṭnī (1891)
4	Ibn ʿUmar	Dāraquṭnī (1887)
5	Umm Saʿd al-Anṣāriyyah	Ṭabarānī, *Kabīr* (331)

The Book of Fasting

٤٧ - أَفْطَرَ الْحَاجِمُ وَالْمَحْجُومُ.

47. 'The cupper and the cupped both break their fasts.'[1]

	Narrator	*Compiler(s)*
1	Thawbān	Tirmidhī (774), Nasā'ī, *As-Sunan al-Kubrā* (3120), Ibn Mājah (1680), Abū Dāwūd (2367) and Ḥākim (1558)
2	Shaddād ibn Aws	Abū Dāwūd (2369) and Ḥākim (1563)
3	Rāfi' Ibn Khadīj	Tirmidhī (774) and Ḥākim (1561)
4	'Alī	Nasā'ī, *As-Sunan al-Kubrā* (3149)
5	Usāmah Ibn Zayd	Nasā'ī, *As-Sunan al-Kubrā* (3153)
6	Bilāl	Nasā'ī, *As-Sunan al-Kubrā* (3144)
7	Ma'qal Ibn Yasār	Nasā'ī, *As-Sunan al-Kubrā* (3154)
8	Abū Mūsā	Nasā'ī, *As-Sunan al-Kubrā* (3195)
9	Abū Hurayrah	Nasā'ī, *As-Sunan al-Kubrā* (3163)

1 Sharaf al-Ḥaqq says in 'Awn al-Ma'būd: 'Khaṭṭābī said: "People have differed about the interpretation of this hadith. A group of the people of knowledge is of the opinion that cupping breaks the fast according to the obvious sense of the hadith. This is the opinion of Aḥmad ibn Ḥanbal and Isḥāq ibn Rāhawayh. They said: 'He must make up the fast but does not have to do penance.'"

Masrūq, Ḥasan, and Ibn Sīrīn were of the opinion that the fasting person should not cup, and Awzā'ī used to dislike it. Ibn al-Musayyib, Sha'bī and Nakha'ī said: "Cupping is disliked for the fasting person because of the weakness it causes." Among those who did not use to see any harm in cupping for the fasting person are Sufyān ath-Thawrī, Mālik ibn Anas and Shāfi'ī; and that is the opinion of Abū Ḥanīfah and his companions.'

10	ʿĀʾishah	Nasāʾī, *As-Sunan al-Kubrā* (3120)
11	Anas	Bazzār[1]
12	Jābir	Bazzār (4970)
13	Samurah	Bazzār (4568)
14	Ibn ʿAbbās	Bazzār (4970)
15	Ibn ʿUmar	Ṭabarānī, *Awsaṭ* (6139)

٤٨ - لَيْسَ مِنْ الْبِرِّ الصَّوْمُ فِي السَّفَرِ.

48. 'Fasting while traveling is not from piety.'

	Narrator	*Compiler(s)*
1	Jābir ibn ʿAbdillāh	Būkhārī (1946) and Muslim (1115)
2	Kaʿb ibn ʿĀṣim al-Ashʿarī	Aḥmad (23680)[2]
3	Abū Barzah al-Aslamī	Aḥmad[3]
4	Ibn ʿAbbās	Ṭabarānī, *Kabīr* (11447)
5	Ibn ʿUmar	Ṭabarānī, *Awsaṭ* (6293)
6	ʿAmmār ibn Yāsir	Ṭabarānī[4]
7	Abu ad-Dardāʾ	Ṭabarānī, *Awsaṭ* (9193)

٤٩ - صَوْمُ يَوْمِ عَاشُورَاءَ يُكَفِّرُ سَنَةً وَصَوْمُ يَوْمِ عَرَفَةَ يُكَفِّرُ سَنَتَيْنِ.

49. 'Fasting the Day of *ʿĀshūrāʾ* atones for the sins of a year and fasting the Day of ʿArafah atones for the sins of two years.'

	Narrator	*Compiler(s)*
1	Abū Qatādah	Muslim (1162)
2	Qatādah ibn an-Nuʿmān	Ibn Mājah (1731)

1 Abū Yaʿlā, *Muʿjam* (269).

2 Shāfiʿī has related a hadith in his *Musnad* wherein the Prophet ﷺ said this hadith in a different dialect: لَيْسَ مِنَ امْبِرِّ امْصِيَامُ فِي امْسَفَرِ which replaces the definite article *alif lām* with *alif mīm* (p.57).

3 Ṭabarānī, *Awsaṭ* (5597).

4 Haythamī, *Majmaʿ* (4929).

3	Ibn ʿUmar	Nasāʾī, *As-Sunan al-Kubrā* (2841)
4	Abū Saʿīd	Bazzār[1]
5	ʿĀʾishah	Aḥmad (24970)
6	Zayd ibn Arqam	Ṭabarānī, *Kabīr* (5089)
7	Sahl ibn Saʿd	Ṭabarānī, *Kabīr* (5923)

٥٠ - مَنْ صَامَ رَمَضَانَ وَأَتْبَعَهُ سِتًّا مِنْ شَوَّالٍ فَكَأَنَّمَا صَامَ الدَّهْرَ.

50. 'Whoever fasts during Ramaḍān, and then follows it up with fasting for six days in Shawwāl, it is as if he has fasted perpetually.'

	Narrator	*Compiler(s)*
1	Abū Ayyūb	Muslim (1164)
2	Thawbān	Nasāʾī, *As-Sunan al-Kubrā* (2873) and Ibn Mājah (1715)
3	Jābir Ibn ʿAbdillāh	Aḥmad (14302)
4	Abū Hurayrah	Bazzār (8334)
5	Ibn ʿAbbās	Ṭabarānī, *Awsaṭ* (4642)
6	Ibn ʿUmar	Ṭabarānī, *Awsaṭ* (8622)
7	Ghannām	Ṭabarānī[2]
8	Barāʾ ibn ʿĀzib	Dāraquṭnī[3]

٥١ - أَيَّامُ التَّشْرِيقِ أَيَّامُ أَكْلٍ وَشُرْبٍ.

51. 'The Days of *Tashrīq* are days of eating and drinking.'[4]

	Narrator	*Compiler(s)*
1	Kaʿb ibn Mālik	Muslim (1142)
2	Nubayshah al-Hudhalī	Muslim (1141)

1 Ṭabarānī, *Awsaṭ* (2065).
2 Haythamī, *Majmaʿ* (5104).
3 Khallāl, *Majālis* (67).
4 These are the three days following ʿĪd al-Aḍḥā.

3	ʿUqbah ibn ʿĀmir	Ḥākim (1586)
4	ʿAlī	Ḥākim (1588)
5	Umm Masʿūd Ibn al-Ḥakam az-Zurqī	Ḥākim (1588)
6	ʿAbdullāh ibn Ḥudhāfah as-Sahmī	Ibn ʿAsākir (27:346)[1]
7	Umm al-Faḍl bint al-Ḥārith	Ibn ʿAsākir (27:347)[2]
8	Abū Hurayrah	Ibn Mājah (1719)
9	Bishr ibn Suḥaym al-Fafārī	Ibn Mājah (1720)
10	Saʿd ibn Abī Waqqāṣ	Aḥmad (1456)
11	Ibn ʿUmar	Aḥmad (4970)
12	Budayl ibn al-Warqāʾ	Aḥmad (24009/15)
13	Ibn ʿAbbās	Ṭabarānī, *Kabīr* (11203)
14	Maʿmar ibn ʿAbdillāh al-ʿAdawī	Ṭabarānī, *Kabīr* (1093)
15	ʿUmar ibn al-Khaṭṭāb	Ṭabarānī, *Awsaṭ* (7236)
16	Usāmah al-Hudhalī	Ṭabarānī, *Awsaṭ* (7180)

1 Mālik (1393).

2 Ṭabarānī, *Awsaṭ* (6601).

The Book of the Hajj

٥٢ - عُمْرَةٌ فِي رَمَضَانَ تَعْدِلُ حَجَّةً.

52. 'To make the minor pilgrimage during Ramaḍān is equivalent to Hajj.'

	Narrator	*Compiler(s)*
1	Jābir ibn ʿAbdillāh	Būkhārī (1863)[1]
2	Yūsuf ibn ʿAbdillāh ibn Salām	Tirmidhī[2]
3	Umm Maʿqil	Tirmidhī (939)
4	Ibn ʿAbbās	Tirmidhī (939)
5	Wahb Ibn Ḥubaysh	Tirmidhī (939)
6	Abū Maʿqil	Tirmidhī[3]
8	ʿAlī	Bazzār (636)
9	Anas	Ṭabarānī, *Kabīr* (722)
10	Ibn az-Zubayr	Ṭabarānī, *Kabīr* (271)
11	ʿUrwah al-Bāriqī	Ṭabarānī, *Kabīr* (403)
12	Abū Ṭulayq	Ṭabarānī, *Kabīr* (425)
13	Aḥmadī	Baghawī and Ibn Qāniʿ
14	Bakr ibn Abdillāh al-Ḥuzanī (NCM)	Saʿīd ibn Manṣūr, *Sunan*[4]

1 Bukhārī has also recorded this hadith from Ibn ʿAbbās (1782).

2 Ibn Abī Shaybah (13027).

3 Ibn Abī Shaybah (771).

4 Abū Dāwūd has related this hadith with the Companion Ibn ʿAbbās (1990).

The Book of Etiquette

٥٣ - الْمُسْتَشَارُ مُؤْتَمَنٌ.

53. 'The advisor is in a position of trust.'

	Narrator	*Compiler(s)*
1	Abū Hurayrah	Tirmidhī (2822), Nasā'ī (6583), Ibn Mājah (3745) and Abū Dāwūd (5128)
2	Umm Salamah	Tirmidhī (2823)
3	Ibn ʿUmar	Ḥākim (7178)
4	Abū Saʿīd	Aḥmad
5	ʿAlī	Ṭabarānī, *Awsaṭ* (2195)
6	Jābir ibn Samurah	Ṭabarānī, *Awsaṭ* (5879)
7	Samurah ibn Jundub	Ṭabarānī, *Kabīr* (6914)
8	Nuʿmān ibn Bashīr	Ṭabarānī[1]
9	Abū 'l-Haytham ibn at-Tayhān	Ṭabarānī, *Kabīr* (573)
10	Ibn az-Zubayr	Ṭabarānī, *Kabīr* (302)
12	Ibn ʿAbbās	Kharā'iṭī, *Makārim al-Akhlāq* (781)

٥٤ - اتَّقُوا النَّارَ وَلَوْ بِشِقِّ تَمْرَةٍ.

54. 'Save yourselves from the Fire even with only half a date!'

---

1 Ṭaḥāwī, *Sharḥ Mushkil al-Āthār* (4295).

	Narrator	*Compiler(s)*
1	ʿAdī ibn Ḥātim	Būkhārī (1417) and Muslim (1016)
2	Ibn Masʿūd	Aḥmad (3679)
3	ʿĀ'ishah	Aḥmad (25057)
4	Abū Bakr aṣ-Ṣiddīq	Bazzār (82)
5	Anas	Bazzār (6619)
6	Nuʿmān ibn Bashīr	Bazzār (3226)
7	Abū Hurayrah	Bazzār (9586)
8	Ibn ʿAbbās	Ṭabarānī, *Kabīr* (12771)
9	Abū Umāmah	Ṭabarānī, *Kabīr* (8017)
10	ʿAbdullāh ibn Mukhaymir	Ṭabarānī
11	Faḍālah ibn ʿUbayd	Ṭabarānī, *Kabīr* (777)
12	Ibn ʿUmar	Ibn Asākir, *Tārīkh* (12454)
13	ʿUrwah ibn az-Zubayr (NCM)	Ibn Jarīr in his commentary on the Qur'an (19:410)
14	Qatādah (NCM)	Ibn Jarīr in his commentary on the Qur'an (19:410–411)
15	Ḥasan (NCM)	Saʿīd ibn Manṣūr, *Sunan*[1]

٥٥ - لَا حَوْلَ وَلَا قُوَّةَ إِلَّا بِاللهِ كَنْزٌ مِنْ كُنُوزِ الْجَنَّةِ.

55. 'There is no power nor strength except with Allah,' is a treasure from the treasures of Paradise.'

	Narrator	*Compiler(s)*
1	Abū Mūsā al-Ashʿarī	Būkhārī (4205) and Muslim (2704)
2	Abū Dharr	Nasā'ī, *As-Sunan al-Kubrā* (9758) and Ibn Mājah (3825)
3	Abū Hurayrah	Ḥākim (54)
4	Zayd ibn Thābit	Ibn Abī Shaybah (136)
5	Muʿādh ibn Jabal	Ibn Abī Shaybah (35265)

1 Ṭabarānī in *Kabīr* (354) has mentioned this hadith with the Companion ʿImrān ibn Ḥuṣayn.

6	Abū Ayyūb al-Anṣārī	Ibn Abī Shaybah (35262)
7	Qays ibn Saʿd ibn ʿUbādah	Bazzār (3742) and Ḥākim (7787)
8	Ḥāzim ibn Ḥarmalah	Ṭabarānī, *Kabīr* (1642)
9	Zayd Ibn Isḥāq al-Anṣārī	Ṭabarānī, *Kabīr* (5151)
10	Muʿāwiyah ibn Ḥaydah[1]	Ṭabarānī, *Kabīr* (996)
11	Faḍālah Ibn ʿUbayd	Ṭabarānī, *Kabīr* (773)
12	Abu ad-Dardā'	Ṭabarānī, *Duʿā'* (1662)
13	Anas	Abū Nuʿaym
14	Abū Bakr aṣ-Ṣiddīq	Ibn ʿAsākir (2168)

٥٦ - لَأَنْ يَمْتَلِئَ جَوْفُ أَحَدِكُمْ قَيْحًا خَيْرٌ لَهُ مِنْ أَنْ يَمْتَلِئَ شِعْرًا.

56. 'It is better for you to fill your belly with pus than to fill it with poetry.'

	Narrator	*Compiler(s)*
1	Abū Hurayrah	Būkhārī (6155) and Muslim (2257)
2	Ibn ʿUmar	Būkhārī (6154)
3	Saʿd Ibn Abī Waqqāṣ	Muslim (2258)
4	Abū Saʿīd al-Khudrī	Muslim (2259)
5	ʿUmar	Abū ʿUwānah[2]
6	Salmān al-Fārisī	Ṭabarānī, *Kabīr* (6132)
7	ʿUtbah Ibn ʿAbd as-Sulamī	Ṭabarānī
8	Ibn Masʿūd	Ṭabarānī (9752)
9	ʿAwf Ibn Mālik	Ṭabarānī, *Kabīr* (144)
10	Mālik Ibn ʿUmayr	Ṭabarānī, *Kabīr* (655)
11	Abu ad-Dardā'	Ṭabarānī[3]
12	Jābir ibn ʿAbdillāh	Abū Yaʿlā (2056)
13	Ibn ʿAbbās	Ibn ʿAdī[4]

1 He is the grandfather of Bahz ibn Ḥakīm.

2 Bazzār (247).

3 Tirmidhī lists Abu ad-Dardā' among the narrators of this hadith (2851).

4 Muttaqī al-Hindī, *Kanz* (8926).

14	ʿĀʾishah	Ibn ʿAdī[1]
15	Ḥasan (NCM)	Abū ʿUbayd
16	Shaʿbī (NCM)	Abū ʿUbayd[2]

٥٧ - لَوْ كَانَ لِابْنِ آدَمَ وَادِيًا مِنْ ذَهَبٍ لَأَحَبَّ أَنْ يَكُونَ إِلَيْهِ الثَّانِيَ وَلَوْ كَانَ لَهُ الثَّانِي لَأَحَبَّ أَنْ يَكُونَ لَهُ الثَّالِث وَلَا يَمْلَأُ جَوْفَ ابْنِ آدَمَ إِلَّا التُّرَابُ وَيَتُوبُ اللهُ عَلَى مَنْ تَابَ.

57. 'If the son of Ādam had a valley of gold, he would love to have a second; and if he had a second, he would love to have a third. Nothing fills the son of Ādam's belly except dust, and Allah turns to whoever repents.'

	Narrator	*Compiler(s)*
1	Anas	Bukhārī (6439)
2	Ibn az-Zubayr	Bukhārī (6438)
3	Ibn ʿAbbās	Bukhārī (6436)
4	Ubayy ibn Kaʿb	Tirmidhī (3793)
5	Buraydah	Bazzār (4433)
6	Abū Saʿīd al-Khudri	Bazzār (3637)[3]
7	Samurah	Bazzār (3635)[4]
8	ʿĀʾishah	Bazzār (3640)[5]
9	Jābir ibn Abdillāh	Aḥmad (14657) and Abū ʿUbayd, *Faḍāʾil*
10	Zayd ibn Arqam	Aḥmad (19280) and Abū ʿUbayd in *Faḍāʾil*
11	Abū Mūsā al-Ashʿarī	Abū ʿUbayd[6]

1 Ṭaḥāwī, *Sharḥ Maʿānī* (6988).
2 Ṭaḥāwī, *Sharḥ Maʿānī* (6989).
3 Haythamī, *Kashf al-Astār* (3637).
4 Ibid.
5 Ibid.
6 Muslim (119).

12	Saʿd ibn Abī Waqqāṣ	Ṭabarānī, *Awsaṭ* (3473)
13	Abū Wāqid al-Laythī	Ṭabarānī, *Awsaṭ* (2446)
14	Abū Umāmah	Ṭabarānī, *Kabīr* (7970)
15	Kaʿb ibn ʿIyāḍ al-Ashʿarī	Ṭabarānī, *Kabīr* (406)

٥٨ - إِنَّ أَحَدَكُمْ لَيَعْمَلُ بِعَمَلِ أَهْلِ الْجَنَّةِ. . .

58. 'Indeed, one of you does the deeds of the people of Paradise. . .'[1]

	Narrator	*Compiler(s)*
1	Ibn Masʿūd	Būkhārī (3208) and Muslim (2463)
2	Anas	Būkhārī[2]
3	Sahl ibn Saʿd	Būkhārī (6607)
4	Ḥudhayfah ibn Usayd	Muslim (2645)[3]
5	Abū Hurayrah	Muslim (2651)
6	ʿAlī	Ṭabarānī[4]
7	Ibn ʿUmar[5]	Ṭabarānī, *Awsaṭ* (8801)
8	Aktham ibn Abī 'l-Jawn	Ṭabarānī, *Kabīr* (872)
9	ʿĀ'ishah	Aḥmad (24762)
10	Ibn ʿUmar	Bazzār[6]
11	ʿUrs ibn ʿUmayrah	Bazzār[7]
12	Jābir	Firyābī, *Tārīkh*[8]
13	Abū Dharr	Firyābī, *Tārīkh*[9]

1 See appendix for a variation of the hadith.

2 Aḥmad (13695).

3 Muslim quotes a hadith from Ḥudhayfah which contains the same basic meaning of destiny but it is not this same hadith.

4 Ibn ʿAbd al-Barr, *Jāmiʿ* (1881).

5 Ṭabarānī has related a variation of this hadith from ʿAbdullāh ibn ʿAmr in the reference above.

6 Lālakā'ī, *Sharḥ Uṣūl Iʿtiqād* (1088).

7 Ṭabarānī, *Ṣaghīr* (512).

8 Firyābī, *Qadr* (143). Jābir's hadith has a smillar meaning.

9 Firyābī, *Qadr* (123). Abū Dharr's hadith has a smillar meaning.

14	Rabāḥ al-Lakhmī	Ibn Marduwayh, *Tafsīr*
15	Mālik ibn al-Ḥuwayrith	Abū Nuʿaym, *Ṭibb*
16	Ibn ʿAbbās	Mulakhkhaṣ, *Fawāʾid*

٥٩ - كُلُّ مَعْرُوفٍ صَدَقَةٌ.

59. 'Every act of courtesy is an act of charity.'

	Narrator	*Compiler(s)*
1	Jābir ibn ʿAbdillāh	Būkhārī (6021)
2	Ḥudhayfah	Būkhārī, *Al-Adab al-Mufrad* (233)
3	ʿAbdullāh ibn Zayd al-Khaṭmī[1]	Būkhārī, *Al-Adab al-Mufrad* (231)
4	Ibn Masʿūd	Ṭabarānī, *Awsaṭ* (9044)
5	Nubayṭ ibn Shurayṭ	Ṭabarānī, *Ṣaghīr* (64)
6	Ibn Masʿūd al-Anṣārī	Ṭabarānī, *Kabīr* (639)
7	Thābit's father	Ṭabarānī, *Kabīr* (964)
8	Abū Mālik al-Ashjaʿī's father	Ṭabarānī, *Kabīr* (8200)

٦٠ - نَزَلَ الْقُرْآنُ عَلَى سَبْعَةِ أَحْرُفٍ.

60. 'The Qur'an was revealed on seven letters.'[2]

	Narrator	*Compiler(s)*
1	Ibn ʿUmar[3]	[Bukhārī (2419) and Muslim (818)]
2	ʿUthmān	
3	Ubayy ibn Kaʿb	[Muslim (820)]
4	Anas	[Aḥmad (21132)]
5	Ḥudhayfah ibn al-Yamān	[Bazzār (2908) and Aḥmad (23273)]
6	Zayd ibn Arqam	
7	Samurah ibn Jundub	[Aḥmad (20179)]

1 Aḥmad and others have ʿAbdullāh ibn Yazīd al-Khaṭmī (18741).
2 See appendix for a variation of the hadith.
3 Bukhārī quotes the hadith from ʿUmar ibn al-Khaṭṭab.

8	Sulaymān ibn Ṣard	[Aḥmad (21149)]
9	Ibn ʿAbbās	[Bukhārī (4991) and Muslim (819)]
10	Ibn Masʿūd	[Bazzār (2081)]
11	ʿAbd ar-Raḥmān ibn ʿAwf	
12	ʿUmar ibn Abī Salamah	[Ṭabarānī, *Kabīr* (8296)]
13	ʿAmr ibn al-ʿĀṣ	[Aḥmad (17819)]
14	Muʿādh ibn Jabal	[Ṭabarānī, *Kabīr* (312)]
15	Hishām ibn al-Ḥakam	
16	Abū Bakrah	[Bazzār (3622) and Aḥmad (20425)]
17	Abū Jahm[1]	[Aḥmad (17542)]
18	Abū Saʿīd al-Khudrī	[Ṭabarānī, *Awsaṭ* (6033)]
19	Abū Ṭalḥah al-Anṣārī	
20	Abū Hurayrah	[Bazzār (8010) and Aḥmad (7989)]
21	Umm Ayyūb	[Aḥmad (27443)]

٦١ - قُلْ هُوَ اللهُ أَحَدٌ تَعْدِلُ ثُلُثَ الْقُرْآنِ.

61. ‘[The chapter:] *Say: He is Allah, the One*, amounts to a third of the Qur’an.’

	Narrator	*Compiler(s)*
1	Abū Saʿīd	Būkhārī (5013)
2	Abu ad-Dardā’	Muslim (811)
3	Abū Hurayrah	Muslim (812)
4	Abū Ayyūb	Tirmidhī and Nasā’ī, *As-Sunan al-Kubrā* (10455)
5	Abū Masʿūd	Nasā’ī, *As-Sunan al-Kubrā* (10411); and Ibn Mājah (3789)
6	Ubayy Ibn Kaʿb	Aḥmad[2]
7	Ibn ʿUmar	Aḥmad[3]

1 Aḥmad has quoted it from Abū Juhaym.

2 Nasā’ī, *As-Sunan al-Kubrā* (10453).

3 Ṭabarānī, *Awsaṭ* (186).

8	Umm Kulthūm bint ʿUqbah ibn Abī Muʿayṭ	Aḥmad (27274)
9	Anas	Abū Yaʿlā (4118)
10	Jābir ibn ʿAbdillāh	Bazzār[1]
11	Saʿd ibn Abī Waqqāṣ[2]	Ṭabarānī[3]
12	Ibn ʿUmar	Ṭabarānī, *Awsaṭ* (186)
13	Ibn Masʿūd	Ṭabarānī, *Awsaṭ* (741)
14	Muʿādh ibn Jabal	Ṭabarānī, *Kabīr* (223)
15	Ibn ʿAbbās	Abū ʿUbayd, *Faḍāʾil al-Qurʾān* (p.268)
16	Qatādah ibn an-Nuʿmān	Bayhaqī, *Sunan*[4]

٦٢ - الْمَرْءُ مَعَ مَنْ أَحَبَّ.

62. 'A person is with whom he loves.'

	Narrator	*Compiler(s)*
1	Abū Mūsā	Būkhārī (6170) and Muslim (2641)
2	Ṣafwān ibn ʿAssāl	Tirmidhī (2387)
3	Jābir Ibn ʿAbdillāh	Aḥmad (1054)
4	ʿAbdullāh ibn Masʿūd	Aḥmad (3718)
5	ʿAlī	Bazzār (746)
6	Abū Qatādah	Ṭabarānī, *Awsaṭ* (107)
7	Abū Sarīḥah	Ṭabarānī, *Kabīr* (3061)
8	ʿAbdullāh ibn Yazīd al-Khaṭmī	Ṭabarānī[5]
9	Ṣafwān ibn Qudāmah	Ṭabarānī, *Awsaṭ* (2001)
10	ʿUrwah ibn Muḍarris aṭ-Ṭāʾī	Ṭabarānī, *Awsaṭ* (2206)
11	Muʿādh ibn Jabal	Ṭabarānī, *Kabīr* (138)
12	Abū Umāmah al-Bāhilī	Ṭabarānī, *Awsaṭ* (6620)

1 Haythamī, *Kashf al-Astār* (2299).

2 Ṭabarānī has related this hadith from Saʿd ibn Mālik in *Ṣaghīr* (165) and so has Bazzār (1211).

3 Haythamī, *Majmaʿ* (11540).

4 Bayhaqī, *Shuʿab* (2302).

5 Haythamī in *Majmaʿ* (18026).

٦٣ - مَنْ رَآنِي فِي الْمَنَامِ فَقَدْ رَآنِي فَإِنَّ الشَّيْطَانَ لَا يَتَمَثَّلُ بِي.

63. 'Whoever has seen me in a dream has surely seen me, for Satan cannot take my form.'

	Narrator	*Compiler(s)*
1	Anas	Būkhārī (6994) and Muslim (6994)
2	Abū Saʿīd	Būkhārī (6997) and Muslim (6997)
3	Abū Qatādah	Būkhārī (6995) and Muslim (2267)
4	Abū Hurayrah	Būkhārī (110) and Muslim (2266)
5	Jābir	Muslim (2268)
6	Ibn Masʿūd	Tirmidhī (2276)
7	Ibn ʿAbbās	Ibn Mājah (3905)
8	Abū Juḥayfah	Ibn Mājah (3904)
9	Abū Qatādah	Aḥmad (22606)
10	Abū Mālik al-Ashjaʿī	Aḥmad (15880)
11	Abū Saʿīd	Ṭabarānī, *Awsaṭ* (3026)
12	Ibn ʿAmr	Ṭabarānī, *Awsaṭ* (608)
13	Abū Bakrah	Ṭabarānī[1]
14	Mālik ibn ʿAbdillāh al-Kathʿamī	Ṭabarānī, *Kabīr* (660)
15	Ṭāriq ibn Ashyam al-Ashja'ī	Būkhārī, *Tārīkh* (3113)

٦٤ - الرُّؤْيَا الصَّالِحَةِ جُزْءٌ مِنْ سِتَّةٍ وَأَرْبَعِينَ جُزْءًا مِنَ النُّبُوَّةِ.

64. 'The true dream is a part from the forty-six parts of prophecy.' There are variant narrations in which 'fifty parts,' 'seventy parts' and 'forty parts' are mentioned.

	Narrator	*Compiler(s)*
1	Abū Hurayrah	Būkhārī (6988)
2	Ibn ʿAbbās	Aḥmad (2894)
3	Ibn ʿUmar	Aḥmad (4678)
4	ʿAbdullāh ibn ʿAmr	Aḥmad (7044)

1 Ibn Kathīr, *Jāmiʿ al-Masānīd* (11655).

5	Jābir	Aḥmad (14681)
6	ʿAbbās ibn ʿAbd al-Muṭṭalib	Ṭabarānī, *Awsaṭ* (5812)
7	Samurah	Ṭabarānī, *Kabīr* (7057)
8	Ibn Masʿūd	Ṭabarānī, *Ṣaghīr* (928)
9	Anas	Ṭabarānī, *Awsaṭ* (5891)
10	ʿAwf ibn Mālik	Bazzār (2743)
11	ʿUbādah Ibn Ṣāmit	Abū Dāwūd (5018)

٦٥ - لا يَحِلُّ لِمُسْلِمٍ أَنْ يَهْجُرَ أَخَاهُ فَوْقَ ثَلاثٍ.

65. 'It is not permissible for a Muslim to avoid his brother for more than three days.'[1]

	Narrator	*Compiler(s)*
1	Anas	Būkhārī (6076) and Muslim (2558)
2	Abū Ayyūb al-Anṣārī	Būkhārī (6077) and Muslim (2560)
3	Saʿd ibn Abī Waqqāṣ	Aḥmad (1589)
4	Hishām ibn ʿĀmir	Aḥmad (16257)
5	Ibn ʿAbbās	Ṭabarānī, *Awsaṭ* (3030)
6	Ibn ʿUmar	Ṭabarānī, *Awsaṭ* (7032)
7	Ibn Masʿūd	Ṭabarānī, *Awsaṭ* (2610)
8	Abū Hurayrah	Abū Dāwūd (4912)
9	ʿĀ'ishah	Abū Dāwūd (4913)

٦٦ - الدُّنْيَا خَضِرَةٌ حُلْوَةٌ.

66. 'The world is lush and sweet.'

	Narrator	*Compiler(s)*
1	Ḥakīm ibn Ḥizām	Būkhārī (1472) and Muslim (1035)
2	Abū Saʿīd	Būkhārī (1465) and Muslim (1052)

1 This is in the case of him not having a legislated excuse such as open sinfulness or heresy.

3	Khawlah bint Qays	Tirmidhī (2374)
4	Zayd ibn Thābit	Ṭabarānī, *Kabīr* (4872)
5	Ibn ʿAmrah[1]	Ṭabarānī (850)
6	ʿAbd ar-Raḥmān ibn Abī Samurah	Ṭabarānī[2]
7	Abū Bakrah	Ṭabarānī[3]
8	Abū Hurayrah	Ṭabarānī[4]
9	Umm Salamah	Ṭabarānī, *Awsaṭ* (8359)
10	Maymūnah	Ṭabarānī, *Kabīr* (58)
11	ʿAmrah bint al-Ḥārith	Ṭabarānī, *Kabīr* (850)
12	Anas	Bazzār (6396)
13	ʿĀ'ishah	Bazzār[5]

٦٧ - مَنْ لَا يَرْحَمُ لَا يُرْحَمُ.

67. 'No mercy will be had on he who has no mercy.'

	Narrator	*Compiler(s)*
1	Jarīr al-Bajalī	Būkhārī (6013) and Muslim (2319)
2	Abū Hurayrah	Būkhārī (5997) and Muslim (2318)
3	Abū Saʿīd	Aḥmad (11362)
4	Jarīr	Ṭabarānī, *Awsaṭ* (1713)
5	Ibn ʿUmar	Ṭabarānī, *Kabīr* (13488)
6	Ibn Masʿūd	Ṭabarānī, *Ṣaghīr* (281)
7	Ashʿath ibn Qays	Ṭabarānī (6188)
8	Muʿāwiyah ibn Ḥaydah	Ṭabarānī, *Awsaṭ* (4168)
9	ʿImrān ibn Ḥuṣayn	Bazzār (3562)

1 Ṭabarānī quotes this hadith from ʿAmr's nephew, Muḥammad ibn ʿAbd ar-Raḥmān ibn al-Ḥārith ibn Abī Ḍirār, who relates it from ʿAmrah.

2 Haythamī, *Majmaʿ* (17803).

3 Haythamī, *Majmaʿ* (17807).

4 Haythamī, *Majmaʿ* (17810).

5 Haythamī, *Majmaʿ* (17809).

This hadith has also been related from Muʿāwiyah, as recorded by Ṭabarānī, *Kabīr* (816).

٦٨ - حَدِيثُ الْقَبْضَتَيْنِ فِي ذُرِّيَّةِ آدَمَ، حَدِيْثُ يَوْمِ الْمِيثَاقِ: هؤُلَاءِ فِي الْجَنَّةِ وَ لَا أُبَالِي.

68. The hadith of the two handfuls of the progeny of Ādam, on the day of the Pledge [when it will be said], 'These are in Paradise and I do not care.'[1]

	Narrator	*Compiler(s)*
1	Anas	Bazzār[2]
2	ʿUmar	Mālik (3337), Tirmidhī (3075), Abū Dāwūd (4703) and Ḥākim
3	ʿAlī	Firyābī in *Qadr* (35)[3]

٦٩ - مَا بَيْنَ بَيْتِي وَمِنْبَرِي رَوْضَةٌ مِنْ رِيَاضِ الْجَنَّةِ.

69. 'What is between my house and my pulpit is a garden from the gardens of Paradise.'

	Narrator	*Compiler(s)*
1	Abū Hurayrah	Būkhārī (1109) and Muslim (1391)
2	ʿAbdullāh ibn Zayd al-Māzinī	Muslim (1390) [and Bukhārī (1195)]
3	Jābir ibn ʿAbdillāh	Ibn ʿAsākir (2646)
4	Abū Bakr aṣ-Ṣiddīq	Abū Bakr ash-Shāfiʿī, *Fawāʾid* (106); and Ibn ʿAsākir (9770)[4]

1 See appendix for a variation of the hadith.

2 Abū Yaʿlā al-Mūṣilī (3422).

3 This hadith has also been related by Muʿādh ibn Jabal in Aḥmad (22077); Abū Mūsā in Firyābī (35); ʿAbdullāh ibn ʿAmr in Bayhaqī, *Asmāʾ* (713); Abū Bakr aṣ-Ṣiddīq in Bayhaqī, *Qaḍāʾ* (462); Abū Saʿīd in Ibn Khuzaymah, *Tawḥīd* 1:186; Ibn ʿUmar in Bazzār (5833); Abu ad-Dardāʾ in Aḥmad (27488); Abū Qatādah as-Sulamī in Aḥmad (17660); and Hishām ibn Ḥakīm ibn Ḥizām in Ṭabarānī, *Kabīr* (434).

4 This hadith has also been related by Abū Saʿīd in Aḥmad (11003); ʿAlī in Tirmidhī (3915); Umm Salamah in Nasāʾī, *As-Sunan al-Kubrā* (4276); ʿUmar in Abū Nuʿaym, *Ḥilyah*, 3:264; his son Ibn ʿUmar in Ṭaḥāwī, *Sharḥ Mushkil al-Āthār* (2873); Zubayr ibn al-ʿAwwām in Ṭabarānī, *Awsaṭ* (6444); and Sahl ibn Saʿd in Bayhaqī, *As-Sunan al-Kubrā* (10288).

٧٠ - إِنَّ مِنْ الشِّعْرِ لَحِكْمَةً.

70. 'Indeed some poetry most certainly contains wisdom.'

	Narrator	*Compiler(s)*
1	Ubayy Ibn Kaʿb	Būkhārī (6145), Aḥmad (15786), Abū Dāwūd (5010) and Ibn Mājah (3755)
2	Buraydah ibn al-Ḥaṣīb	Abū Dāwūd (5012)
3	Ibn Masʿūd	Tirmidhī (2844)
4	Ibn ʿAbbās	Tirmidhī (2845), Ibn Mājah (3756) and Bayhaqī, *As-Sunan al-Kubrā* (21100)
5	Anas	Ṭabarānī, *Kabīr* (756)
6	Abū Bakrah	Ṭabarānī, *Awsaṭ* (8304)
7	ʿAmr ibn al-ʿAwf al-Muzanī	Ṭabarānī, *Awsaṭ* (9091)[1]

٧١ - مَنْ عَادَ مَرِيضًا خَاضَ فِي الرَّحْمَةِ حَتَّى يَجْلِسَ، فَإِذَا جَلَسَ غَمَرَتْهُ الرَّحْمَةُ.

71. 'Whoever visits a sick person dives into mercy until he sits, and when he sits, mercy is showered on him.'

	Narrator	*Compiler(s)*
1	Jābir ibn ʿAbdillāh	Aḥmad (14260)
2	Anas	Aḥmad (13673)
3	Kaʿb ibn Mālik	Aḥmad (15797)
4	Abū Umāmah	Aḥmad (22309)
5	ʿAbd ar-Raḥmān ibn ʿAwf	Ṭabarānī[2]
6	ʿAmr ibn Ḥazm	Ṭabarānī, *Awsaṭ* (5296)
7	Ibn ʿAbbās	Ṭabarānī, *Kabīr* (11481)

1 This hadith has also been related by ʿĀʾishah in Bazzār (117) and ʿAbd ar-Raḥmān ibn al-Aswad ibn ʿAbd Yaghūth in Bayhaqī, *As-Sunan al-Kubrā* (21098).

2 Haythamī, *Majmaʿ* (3769).

8	Ṣafwān ibn ʿAssāl	Ṭabarānī, *Kabīr* (7389)
9	Abu ad-Dardā'	Ṭabarānī, *Musnad ash-Shāmiyyīn* (2221)
10	Abū Hurayrah	Ṭabarānī, *Awsaṭ* (2205)

٧٢ - اللَّهُمَّ بَارِكْ لِأُمَّتِي فِي بُكُورِهَا.

72. 'O Allah, bless the mornings for my community!'[1]

	Narrator	*Compiler(s)*
1	Abū Hurayrah	Ibn Mājah (2237)
2	Anas	Bazzār (7523)
3	Ibn ʿAbbās	Bazzār (5242)
4	Jābir ibn ʿAbdillāh	Ṭabarānī, *Awsaṭ* (996)
5	Ibn ʿUmar	Ṭabarānī, *Awsaṭ* (3312)
6	Ibn Masʿūd	Ṭabarānī, *Kabīr* (10490)
7	ʿAbdullāh ibn Salām	Ṭabarānī, *Kabīr* (367)
8	ʿImrān ibn Ḥuṣayn	Ṭabarānī, *Awsaṭ* (5751)
9	Kaʿb ibn Mālik	Ṭabarānī, *Kabīr* (156)
10	Nawwās ibn Samʿān	Ṭabarānī, *Musnad ash-Shāmiyyīn* (458)
11	Nubayṭ ibn Shurayṭ	Ṭabarānī[2]
12	Abū Bakrah	Ṭabarānī, *Awsaṭ* (2975)
13	ʿĀ'ishah	Ṭabarānī, *Awsaṭ* (4829)

٧٣ - مَنْ غَشَّ فَلَيْسَ مِنَّا.

73. 'Whoever deceives is not from us.'

There is a variant wording in which he [ﷺ] says, 'Whoever deceives

1 Some variations specify: 'O Allah, bless the mornings for my community on Thursdays.'

2 Qaḍāʿī, *Musnad ash-Shihāb* (1494).

us.' In most of the paths of transmission the reason he says this is because he saw some (supposedly dry) food in the market that was damp on the inside.

	Narrator	*Compiler(s)*
1	Abū Hurayrah	Būkhārī and Muslim (164)
2	Ibn ʿUmar	Aḥmad (5113)
3	Abū Burdah ibn Dīnār[1]	Aḥmad (15833)
4	Anas	Ṭabarānī, *Awsaṭ* (3773)
5	Barā' ibn ʿĀzib	Ṭabarānī, *Awsaṭ* (4203)
6	Ḥudhayfah	Ṭabarānī, *Awsaṭ* (993)
7	Ibn ʿAbbās	Ṭabarānī, *Kabīr* (11553)
8	Ibn Masʿūd	Ṭabarānī, *Ṣaghīr* (738)
9	Qays ibn Abī Gharazah	Ṭabarān, *Kabīr* (921)
10	Abū Mūsā	Ṭabarānī, *Awsaṭ* (4238)
11	ʿĀ'ishah	Bazzār[2]
12	Ḥārith ibn Suwayd	Ḥākim (2156)

٧٤ - مَنْ بَاعَ عَقَارًا وَلَمْ يَجْعَلْ ثَمَنَهُ فِي مِثْلِهِ لَمْ يُبَارَكْ لَهُ فِيهِ.

74. 'Whoever sells land for higher than the value of its like will not receive any blessing in it.'

	Narrator	*Compiler(s)*
1	Ḥudhayfah ibn al-Yamān	Ibn Mājah (2491)
2	Saʿīd ibn Ḥurayth	Ibn Mājah (2490)
3	Saʿīd ibn Zayd	Aḥmad (1650)
4	ʿImrān ibn Ḥuṣayn	Aḥmad (20002)
5	ʿAmr ibn Ḥurayth	Ṭabarānī, *Kabīr* (5526)
6	Maʿqal ibn Yasār	Ṭabarānī, *Awsaṭ* (8586)
7	Abū Dharr	Ṭabarānī, *Awsaṭ* (7108)

1 Aḥmad lists the Companion as Abū Burdah ibn Niyār.
2 Haythamī, *Majmaʿ* (6340).

٧٥ - الْمُؤْمِنُ يَأْكُلُ فِي مِعًى وَاحِدٍ وَالْكَافِرُ يَأْكُلُ فِي سَبْعَةِ أَمْعَاءٍ.

75. 'The believer eats for one stomach, while the disbeliever eats as if for seven.'

	Narrator	*Compiler(s)*
1	Ibn ʿUmar	Būkhārī (5393) and Muslim (2060)
2	Abū Hurayrah	Būkhārī (5396) and Muslim (2063)
3	Abū Naḍrah[1]	Aḥmad (27226)
4	Naḍlah ibn ʿAmr al-Ghifārī	Aḥmad (18962)
5	A man from Juhaynah	Aḥmad (23135)
6	Maymūnah bint al-Ḥārith	Aḥmad (26845)
7	Anas	Ṭabarānī, *Awsaṭ* (899)
8	Samurah ibn Jundub	Ṭabarānī, *Kabīr* (6959)
9	Sakīn aḍ-Ḍamrī	Ṭabarānī[2]
10	Jahjāh al-Ghifārī	Ṭabarānī, *Kabīr* (2152)
11	Ibn az-Zubayr	Ṭabarānī, *Awsaṭ* (7689)
12	Ibn ʿAmr	Ṭabarānī, *Kabīr* (14682)
13	Abū Saʿīd	Ṭabarānī, *Awsaṭ* (3888)
14	Abū Mūsā	Ṭabarānī[3]

٧٦ - الظُّلْمُ ظُلُمَاتٌ يَوْمَ الْقِيَامَةِ.

76. 'Oppression is gloom on the Day of Resurrection.'

	Narrator	*Compiler(s)*
1	Ibn ʿUmar	Būkhārī (2447) and Muslim (2579)
2	Ibn ʿAmr	Ḥākim (26)
3	Abū Hurayrah	Ḥākim (27)[4]
4	Miswar ibn Makhramah	Ṭabarānī, *Awsaṭ* (6587)

1 Aḥmad lists the Companion as Abū Baṣrah.
2 Ibn Khuzaymah (3064).
3 Muslim (185).
4 Bazzār (8481).

5	Muʿādh ibn Jabal	Ṭabarānī, *Awsaṭ* (3340)
6	Hirmās ibn Ziyād	Ṭabarānī, *Kabīr* (538)[1]

٧٧ - لَنْ يُدْخِلَ أَحَدَكُمُ الْجَنَّةَ عَمَلُهُ، قَالُوا: وَلَا أَنْتَ يَا رَسُولَ اللهِ؟ قَالَ: وَلَا أَنَا إِلَّا أَنْ يَتَغَمَّدَنِيَ اللهُ بِرَحْمَةٍ.

77. 'Deeds will not get any of you into Paradise.' The Companions asked, 'Not even you, O Messenger of Allah?' He replied, 'Not even me, unless Allah envelops me with His mercy.'

	Narrator	*Compiler(s)*
1	Abū Hurayrah	Būkhārī (5673) and Muslim (2816)
2	Abū Saʿīd	Aḥmad (11486)
3	Sharīk ibn Ṭarīf	Ṭabarānī
4	Usāmah ibn Sharīk	Ṭabarānī, *Kabīr* (493)
5	Asad ibn Kurz	Ṭabarānī, *Kabīr* (1001)
6	Abū Mūsā	Ṭabarānī[2]
7	Sharīk ibn Ṭāriq	Bazzār[3]

٧٨ - الْخَيْلُ مَعْقُودٌ بِنَوَاصِيهَا الْخَيْرُ إِلَى يَوْمِ الْقِيَامَةِ.

78. 'Good will remain harnessed to the brow of the steed until the Day of Resurrection.'

	Narrator	*Compiler(s)*
1	Ibn ʿUmar	Būkhārī (2849) and Muslim (96)
2	Abū Hurayrah	Būkhārī and Muslim (26)
3	Anas	Būkhārī (2851) and Muslim (100)
4	ʿUrwah al-Bāriqī	Būkhārī (2850) and Muslim (98)

1 This hadith has also been related by Jābir ibn ʿAbdillāh in Aḥmad (14461).

2 Bazzār (3121).

3 Ṭabarānī, *Kabīr* (7218).

5	Jarīr	Būkhārī and Muslim (97)
6	Jābir ibn ʿAbdillāh	Aḥmad (14791)
7	Abū Dharr	Aḥmad (21570)
8	Abū Saʿīd	Aḥmad (11346)
9	Asmā' bint Zayd[1]	Aḥmad (27574)
10	Ibn al-Ḥanẓaliyyah	Ṭabarānī, *Kabīr* (5623)
11	ʿArīb	Ṭabarānī, *Awsaṭ* (1083)
12	Nuʿmān	Ṭabarānī, *Kabīr* (186)
13	Abū Kabshah	Ṭabarānī, *Kabīr* (849)
14	Abū Umāmah	Ṭabarānī, *Kabīr* (7994)
15	Jarīr ibn Wahb ibn Abī Shaybah from Makḥūl (NCM)	Dāraquṭnī, *Mu'talif*[2]

٧٩ - مَنْ قُتِلَ دُونَ مَالِهِ فَهُوَ شَهِيدٌ.

79. 'Whoever is murdered for his wealth is a martyr.'

The self and family are also mentioned in many paths of its transmission.

	Narrator	*Compiler(s)*
1	Ibn ʿUmar[3]	Muslim (226) [and Bukhārī (2480)]
2	Abū Hurayrah	Muslim (140)
3	Ḥusayn ibn ʿAlī	Aḥmad (590)
4	Ibn ʿAbbās	Aḥmad[4]
5	Saʿd ibn Abī Waqqāṣ	Ṭabarānī, *Awsaṭ* (6810)
6	Anas	Ṭabarānī, *Awsaṭ* (1629)
7	Ibn az-Zubayr	Ṭabarānī, *Kabīr* (290)
8	Ibn Masʿūd	Ṭabarānī, *Kabīr* (10463)

---

1 Aḥmad has recorded Asmā' bint Yazīd.

2 Saʿīd ibn Manṣūr has related this hadith from Makḥūl with a different chain (2429).

3 Muslim and Bukhārī have recorded this hadith from Ibn ʿAmr and not Ibn ʿUmar. Abū Yaʿlā has recorded it from Ibn ʿUmar in *Muʿjam* (p.114).

4 Ṭabarānī, *Kabīr* (12641).

9	ʿAbdullāh ibn ʿĀmir ibn Kurayz	Ṭabarānī, *Awsaṭ* (8069)
10	Shaddād ibn Aws	Ṭabarānī, *Kabīr* (7170)
11	ʿAlī	Ibn Rāhawayh[1]
12	Jābir ibn ʿAbdillāh	Abū Yaʿlā (2061)
13	Suwayd ibn Muqarrin	Ibn ʿAsākir (2550)[2]

٨٠ - غَدْوَةٌ فِي سَبِيلِ اللهِ أَوْ رَوْحَةٌ خَيْرٌ مِنَ الدُّنْيَا وَمَا فِيهَا.

80. 'An early morning or evening foray in the path of Allah is better than the world and whatever is in it.'

	Narrator	*Compiler(s)*
1	Anas	Būkhārī (6568)
2	Abū Ayyūb	Muslim (1883)
3	Sahl ibn Saʿd	Tirmidhī (1648)
4	Ibn ʿAbbās	Tirmidhī (1649)
5	Abū Hurayrah	Ibn Mājah (2755)
6	Muʿāwiyah ibn Khadīj	Aḥmad (27255)
7	Ibn az-Zubayr	Bazzār (987)
8	ʿImrān ibn Ḥuṣayn	Bazzār (3548)

٨١ - لَا تَزَالُ طَائِفَةٌ مِنْ أُمَّتِي ظَاهِرِينَ عَلَى الْحَقِّ حَتَّى يَأْتِيَ أَمْرُ اللهِ.

81. 'There will always be a group from my community who are manifestly upon the truth until the command of Allah comes.'[3]

---

1 Ibn Ḥajar, *Itḥāf al-Maharah* (4317).

2 This hadith has also been related by Saʿīd ibn Zayd, as recorded by Abū Yaʿlā (949).

3 The group referred to is *Ahl as-Sunnah wa'l-Jamāʿah*, the People of the Sunnah and the Group. The *Sunnah* is the words, deeds and tacit approvals of the Prophet ﷺ. The Group is the Companions ﷺ. Thus, the People of the Sunnah and the Group are those who take their religious instruction from the words, deeds and tacit approvals of the Prophet ﷺ as preserved, understood and transmitted by the Companions ﷺ.

	Narrator	*Compiler(s)*
1	Muʿāwiyah ibn Abī Sufyān	Būkhārī (7312) and Muslim (1037)
2	Mughīrah ibn Shuʿbah	Būkhārī (3640) and Muslim (171)
3	Jābir ibn Samurah	Muslim (1922)
4	Muʿādh ibn Jabal	Muslim[1]
5	Jābir ibn ʿAbdillāh	Muslim (1923)
6	Zayd ibn Arqam	Aḥmad (19290)
7	Abū Umāmah	Aḥmad (22320)
8	ʿUmar	Abū Yaʿlā[2]
9	Jābir ibn ʿAbdillāh	Abū Yaʿlā (2078)
10	Abū Hurayrah	Bazzār[3]
11	Murrah al-Bahrī[4]	Ṭabarānī, *Kabīr* (754)
12	Sharjīl ibn as-Samṭ	Ibn ʿAsākir[5]

٨٢ - الْوَلَدُ لِلْفِرَاشِ وَلِلْعَاهِرِ الْحَجَرُ.

82. 'The child is for the bed,[6] and stones are for the adulterer.'

	Narrator	*Compiler(s)*
1	Abū Hurayrah	Būkhārī (6750) and Muslim (1458)
2	ʿUthmān	Būkhārī[7]
3	Ibn ʿAmr	Būkhārī[8]
4	Abū Umāmah	Būkhārī[9]
5	ʿAmr ibn Khārijah	Tirmidhī (1157)

1 Bukhārī (3641).

2 Dārimī (2477).

3 Abū Yaʿlā (6417).

4 Ṭabarānī has Bahzī.

5 Variations of this hadith have also been related by Thawbān in Muslim (170); Ibn ʿAmr in Muslim (176); Saʿd ibn Abī Waqqāṣ in Muslim (177); Qurrah in Bazzār (3303); and ʿImrān ibn Ḥuṣayn in Bazzār (3524).

6 This is a figure of speech indicating that a child is ascribed to the household in which he or she was born.

7 Aḥmad (416).

8 Aḥmad (6933).

9 Ṭabarānī, *Kabīr* (7615).

6	Ibn az-Zubayr	Nasā'ī (3485)
7	Ibn Mas'ūd	Nasā'ī (3486)
8	'Umar ibn al-Khaṭṭāb	Ibn Mājah (2005)
9	'Alī	Aḥmad (820)
10	Ḥasan (NCM)	Aḥmad[1]
11	Sa'd ibn Abī Waqqāṣ	Bazzār (1121)
12	Abū 'Umar	Bazzār[2]
13	Barā' Ibn 'Āzib	Ṭabarānī[3]
14	Zayd ibn Arqam	Ṭabarānī[4]
15	Ibn 'Abbās	Ṭabarānī, *Kabīr* (11434)
16	Ḥusayn ibn 'Alī	Ṭabarān, *Awsaṭ* (5617)
17	'Ubādah Ibn aṣ-Ṣāmit	Ṭabarānī[5]
18	Wāthilah ibn al-Asqa'	Ṭabarānī, *Kabīr* (201)
19	Abū Wā'il (NCM)	Ṭabarānī[6]
20	Mu'āwiyah ibn 'Umar[7]	Abū Ya'lā (791)
21	Anas	Ibn 'Asākir, *Tārīkh*[8]

1 Haythamī, *Ghāyat al-Maqṣad* (2280).

2 I could not find this hadith from Abū 'Umar. Ṭaḥāwī quotes it from Ibn 'Umar in *Sharḥ Ma'ānī* (4676). This could also possibly refer to the narrator Ibn Abī 'Umar, who quotes the hadith in his *Musnad* (Kinānī, *Miṣbāḥ az-Zujājah fī Zawā'id Ibn Mājah* (718)).

3 Ibn al-A'rābī, *Mu'jam* (1643).

4 Ibid.

5 Aḥmad (22778).

6 Ibn Abī Shaybah has recorded this hadith with Abū Wā'il relating from 'Abdullāh ibn Mas'ūd (17692).

7 Mu'āwiyah ibn Abī Sufyān is the one who relates this statement as is clear from the hadith. Perhaps there has been an oversight in the transcription and Suyūṭī listed Mu'awiyah and Ibn 'Umar as two separate narrators. Abū Ḥudhayfah Nabīl ibn Manṣūr al-Kuwaytī, in his reference book of the hadiths in *Fatḥ al-Bārī*, has listed Mu'āwiyah and Ibn 'Umar as two separate narrators of this hadith (*Anīs as-Sārī* (4190)). Ṭaḥāwī quotes it from Ibn 'Umar in *Sharḥ Ma'ānī* (4676).

8 This hadith has also been related by 'Ā'ishah in Bukhārī (6817).

٨٣ - قِصَّةُ مَاعِزٍ فِي الزِّنَا وَرَجْمِهِ.

83. The story of Māʿiz ﷺ, who committed adultery and was stoned.[1]

	Narrator	Compiler(s)
1	Jābir ibn ʿAbdillāh	Bukhārī (5270) and Muslim (17)
2	Ibn ʿAbbās	Bukhārī (6824) and Muslim (1693)
3	Buraydah	Muslim (1695)
4	Jābir ibn Samurah	Muslim (1692)
5	Abū Saʿīd	Muslim (1694)
6	Lajlāj	Abū Dāwūd (4435)
7	Nuʿaym ibn Hazzāl	Abū Dāwūd (4419)
8	Abū Hurayrah	Abū Dāwūd (4428) and Tirmidhī (1428)
9	A man from the Companions	Nasāʾī, *As-Sunan al-Kubrā* (7163)
10	Ibn al-Musayyib	Ibn Mursil[2]
11	Abū Bakr aṣ-Ṣiddīq	Aḥmad (41)
12	Abū Dharr	Aḥmad (21554)
13	Naṣr the father of ʿUthmān	Ibn Abī Shaybah (28781)
14	Abū Barzah al-Aslamī	Ibn Abī Shaybah (28782)
15	ʿAṭāʾ ibn Yasār (NCM)	Ibn Abī Shaybah (28840)
16	Shaʿbī (NCM)	Ibn Abī Shaybah (28770)[3]
17	Abū Umāmah Ibn Sahl ibn Ḥunayf	Abū Qarrah, *Sunnan*[4]

٨٤ - اَلنَّهْيُ عَنِ الشَّفَاعَةِ فِي الْحَدِّ إِذَا بَلَغَ الْإِمَامَ.

84. The prohibition of interceding about a prescribed punishment when the matter has reached the ruler.[5]

1 See appendix for a variation of the hadith.
2 Mālik (3036).
3 Ibn Abī Shaybah also relates this hadith wherein Shaʿbī narrates from Jābir (28766).
4 ʿAbd ar-Razzāq (13339).
5 See appendix for a variation of the hadith.

	Narrator	*Compiler(s)*
1	Jābir ibn ʿAbdillāh	Būkhārī and Muslim (1689)
2	ʿĀʾishah	Būkhārī (3475) and Muslim (1688)
3	Ṣafwān ibn Umayyah	Abū Dāwūd[1]
4	Ibn ʿUmar	Abū Dāwūd[2]
5	Ibn ʿAmr	Abū Dāwūd (4376)
6	Abū Saʿīd	Ḥākim
7	ʿAlī	Abū Yaʿlā (328)
8	Zubayr	Dāraquṭnī (3467)
9	Ibn ʿAbbās	Ibn Abī Shaybah (28084)
10	Ammār ibn Yāsir	Ibn Abī Shaybah (28984)
11	Abū Hurayrah	Ṭabarānī, *Awsaṭ* (8552)
12	Umm Salamah	Ṭabarānī, *Awsaṭ* (7479)
13	Masʿūd ibn al-ʿAjmāʾ	Abū ash-Shaykh, *Kitāb ar-Riqqah*[3]

٨٥ - كُلُّ مُسْكِرٍ حَرَامٌ.

85. ‘Every intoxicant is prohibited.’

	Narrator	*Compiler(s)*
1	ʿĀʾishah	Būkhārī (242) and Muslim (2001)
2	Abū Mūsā	Būkhārī (4343) and Muslim (1733)
3	Ibn ʿAbbās	Abū Dāwūd (3680)
4	Abū Hurayrah	Abū Dāwūd[4]
5	Ibn ʿUmar	Ibn Mājah (3387)
6	Ibn Masʿūd	Ibn Mājah (3388)
7	Muʿāwiyah ibn Abī Sufyān	Ibn Mājah (3389)
8	Abū Mūsā	Nasāʾī (5595)

1 Nasāʾī (4884).

2 Nasāʾī (4890).

3 Aḥmad (23479).
This hadith has also been related from ʿAbdullāh ibn Masʿūd, as quoted by Abū Yaʿlā (5410).

4 Aḥmad (9539).

9	Anas	Aḥmad (12099)
10	ʿUmar	Abū Yaʿlā (248)
11	Khawwāt ibn Jubayr	Ṭabarānī, *Awsaṭ* (1616)
12	Zayd ibn Thābit	Ṭabarānī, *Awsaṭ* (6446)
13	Qays ibn Saʿd	Ṭabarānī, *Kabīr* (898)
14	Abū Saʿīd	Ibn Manīʿ[1]
15	Qurrah ibn Iyās	Bazzār (3316)

٨٦ - إِذَا حَلَفْتَ عَلَى يَمِينٍ فَرَأَيْتَ غَيْرَهَا خَيْرًا مِنْهَا فَكَفِّرْ يَمِينَكَ وَأْتِ الَّذِي هُوَ خَيْرٌ.

86. 'If you swore an oath and then you see something better than what you swore to, absolve your oath and do that which is better.'

	Narrator	*Compiler(s)*
1	ʿAbd ar-Raḥmān ibn Samurah	Būkhārī (6622) and Muslim (1652)
2	Ḥasan[2]	Būkhārī (7146) and Muslim (1651)
3	ʿAdī ibn Ḥātim	Muslim (1651)
4	Ibn ʿAmr	Abū Dāwūd (3274)
5	Udhaynah	Ṭabarānī, *Kabīr* (873)
6	Muʿāwiyah ibn al-Ḥakam	Ṭabarānī, *Awsaṭ* (6987)
7	Umm Salamah	Ṭabarānī, *Kabīr* (694)
8	Abu ad-Dardā'	Ṭabarānī[3]
9	ʿImrān ibn Ḥuṣayn	Ṭabarānī, *Kabīr* (346)

٨٧ - لَا نِكَاحَ إِلَّا بِوَلِيٍّ.

87. 'There is no marriage without a guardian.'

1 Aḥmad (11606).

2 Ḥasan relates from 'Abd ar-Raḥmān ibn Samurah, as quoted by both Bukhārī and Muslim.

3 Tirmidhī lists Abu ad-Dardā' as a narrator of this hadith (1529).

	Narrator	*Compiler(s)*
1	Abū Mūsā	Abū Dāwūd (2085)
2	Ibn ʿAbbās	Ibn Mājah (1880)
3	Jābir	Ṭabarānī, *Awsaṭ* (3926)
4	Abū Hurayrah	Ṭabarānī, *Awsaṭ* (5563)
5	Abū Umāmah	Ṭabarānī, *Kabīr* (8121)
6	ʿĀ'ishah	Ṭabarānī, *Awsaṭ* (6927)
7	ʿImrān ibn Ḥuṣayn	Ṭabarānī, *Kabīr* (299)

٨٨ - النَّهْىُ عَنْ بَيْعِ الْغَرَرِ.

88. The prohibition of transactions based on uncertainty.

	Narrator	*Compiler(s)*
1	Ibn Masʿūd	Muslim and Aḥmad (3676)
2	Sahl ibn Saʿd	Ṭabarānī, *Awsaṭ* (5515)
3	Ibn ʿAbbās	Ṭabarānī, *Kabīr* (11341)
4	Ibn ʿAmr	Ṭabarānī, *Awsaṭ* (8087)
5	ʿAttāb ibn Asīd[1]	Ṭabarānī, *Kabīr* (425)
6	Ibn ʿAmr[2]	Bazzār (5875)
7	Anas	Abū Yaʿlā (2766)

٨٩ - الْوَلَاءُ لِمَنْ أَعْتَقَ.

89. 'Right of inheritance is for he who emancipates.'[3]

	Narrator	*Compiler(s)*
1	ʿĀ'ishah	Būkhārī (456) and Muslim (1504)
2	Ibn ʿAbbās	Bazzār[4]

1 Some historians say his name was ʿAttāb ibn Usayd.

2 Bazzār has Ibn ʿUmar.

3 If a freed slave dies and leaves no family members to inherit from him, then his former master who freed him inherits from him.

4 Ṭabarānī, *Awsaṭ* (607).

3	ʿAlī	Ṭabarānī, *Awsaṭ* (8590)
4	Burayd[1]	Ṭabarānī (525)[2]

٩٠ - الأَئِمَّةُ مِنْ قُرَيْشٍ.

90. 'The leaders are from the Quraysh.'

	Narrator	*Compiler(s)*
1	Abū Barzah	Aḥmad (19777)
2	Anas	Aḥmad (12307)
3	ʿAlī	Ṭabarānī, *Awsaṭ* (3521)[3]

٩١ - لَا هِجْرَةَ بَعْدَ الْفَتْحِ.

91. 'There is no immigration (to Madīnah) after the conquest (of Makkah).'

	Narrator	*Compiler(s)*
1	Mujāshiʿ ibn Masʿūd	Būkhārī (3078) and Muslim (1863)
2	Abū Saʿīd	Aḥmad (11167)
3	Ghazīn[4] ibn al-Ḥārith	Ṭabarānī, *Kabīr* (656)
4	Ḥārith ibn Ghaziyyah	Ṭabarānī, *Kabīr* (3390)[5]

1 Muttaqī al-Hindī in *Kanz* (29636) records the narrator is Buraydah from Ṭabarānī. I could not find this hadith from Burayd or Buraydah. It is possible, however, that the narrator intended here is Barīrah who was the subject of the incident. She narrates this hadith herself as recorded by Ṭabarānī in the reference above.

2 This hadith has also been related by ʿAbdullāh ibn ʿUmar in Aḥmad (4816) and Abū Hurayrah in Muslim (15).

3 Variations of this statement have been related by Aḥmad from Abū Bakr (18), ʿAbdullāh ibn ʿAmr (17808), ʿAbdullāh ibn Masʿūd (4380), Abū Barzah (19777), Abū Masʿūd al-Anṣārī (22355), ʿAbdullāh ibn ʿUmar (4832) and Abū Mūsā al-Ashʿarī (19541). Variations have also been related by Ṭabarānī from ʿAmr ibn ʿAwf ibn Yazīd ibn Milḥah al-Muzanī in *Kabīr* (2), Abū Saʿīd al-Khudrī in *Awsaṭ* (2563) and Muʿāwiyah in *Kabīr* (780), as well as ʿUtbah ibn ʿAbd, by Aḥmad (17654).

4 Ṭabarānī has Ghaziyyah.

5 This hadith has also been related from Ibn ʿAbbās and ʿAbdullāh ibn ʿUmar in

٩٢ - النَّهْيُ عَنْ قَتْلِ النِّسَاءِ وَالصِّبْيَانِ.

92. The prohibition of killing women and children.

	Narrator	Compiler(s)
1	ʿAbdullāh ibn ʿUmar	Bukhārī (305) and Muslim (1744)
2	Ibn ʿAbbās	Aḥmad (3299)
3	Kaʿb ibn Mālik	Ṭabarānī, *Kabīr* (145)
4	ʿAbdullāh ibn ʿAtīk	Ṭabarānī, *Musnad ash-Shāmiyyīn* (1760)
5	Abū Thaʿlabah	Ṭabarānī, *Awsaṭ* (7011)
6	Abū Saʿīd	Ṭabarānī, *Awsaṭ* (4227)

٩٣ - الْحَرْبُ خَدْعَةٌ.

93. 'War is deception.'

	Narrator	Compiler(s)
1	Abū Hurayrah	Bukhārī (3027) and Muslim (1740)
2	ʿAlī	Aḥmad (969)
3	Anas	Aḥmad (13341)
4	Ibn ʿAbbās	Ibn Mājah (2834)
5	Ḥasan ibn ʿAlī	Ṭabarānī, *Kabīr* (2728)
6	Zayd ibn Thābit	Ṭabarānī, *Kabīr* (4866)
7	ʿAwf ibn Mālik	Ṭabarānī, *Kabīr* (95)
8	Nubayṭ ibn Shurayṭ	Ṭabarānī, *Ṣaghīr* (64)
9	Nawwās ibn Samʿān	Ṭabarānī[1]
10	Ḥusayn ibn ʿAlī	Ṭabarānī[2]
11	Ibn ʿUmar	Ṭabarānī[3]
12	ʿAbdullāh ibn Salām	Abū Yaʿlā (7495)

Bukhārī (2783 and 4311), ʿĀ'ishah in Muslim (86) and ʿAbdullāh ibn ʿAmr, Rāfiʿ Ibn Khadīj and Zayd ibn Thābit in Aḥmad (7012 and 21629).

1 Abū ʿUwānah (6551).

2 Bazzār (1344).

3 Bazzār (5412).

13	Khālid ibn al-Walīd	Ibn ʿAsākir (5534)
14	Jābir	Ibn ʿAsākir (28:26)[1]

٩٤ - مَنْ ظَلَمَ قِيدَ شِبْرٍ مِنْ أَرْضٍ طُوِّقَهُ مِنْ سَبْعِ أَرَضِينَ.

94. 'Seven earths will enclose whoever is oppressive even to the extent of a handspan of the ground.'

	Narrator	*Compiler(s)*
1	ʿĀ'ishah	Būkhārī (2453) and Muslim (1612)
2	Ibn Zayd	Aḥmad (1628)
3	Abū Hurayrah	Aḥmad (9019)
4	Yaʿlā ibn Murrah	Aḥmad (17571)
5	Anas	Ṭabarānī, *Awsaṭ* (5519)
6	Saʿd ibn Abī Waqqāṣ	Ṭabarānī, *Awsaṭ* (5149)
7	Ibn ʿAbbās	Ṭabarānī, *Kabīr* (12921)
8	Ḥakam ibn al-Ḥārith as-Sulamī	Ṭabarānī, *Ṣaghīr* (1197)
9	Shaddād ibn Aws	Ṭabarānī, *Kabīr* (7170)
10	Abū Shurayḥ al-Khuzāʿī	Ṭabarānī, *Kabīr* (493)
11	Miswar ibn Makhramah	Ṭabarānī, *Kabīr* (31)
12	ʿUbādah ibn aṣ-Ṣāmit	Ṭabarānī[2]
13	Umayyah (the emancipated slave girl of the Messenger of Allah ﷺ)	Ṭabarānī[3]
14	Ibn ʿUmar	Abū Nuʿaym, *Ḥilyah* (1:96)

1 Aḥmad has also recorded this hadith (14177).

2 Ṭabarānī has quoted a hadith in *Awsaṭ* from ʿUbādah regarding oppression upon the people of Madīnah and its consequences (3589).

3 Muttaqī al-Hindī, *Kanz* (30369).

٩٥ - أَنَّهُ صَلَّى اللهُ عَلَيْهِ وَسَلَّمَ قَضَى بِالشَّاهِدِ وَالْيَمِيْنِ.

95. That He ﷺ judged according to testimony and oaths.[1]

	Narrator	*Compiler(s)*
1	Abū Hurayrah	Abū Dāwūd (3610)
2	Jābir	Ibn Mājah (2369)
3	ʿAmmārah ibn Ḥizām	Aḥmad (37)
4	Bilāl ibn al-Ḥārith	Ṭabarānī, *Kabīr* (1139)
5	Zayd ibn Thārī[2]	Ṭabarānī, *Kabīr* (4909)
6	Ibn ʿUmar[3]	Ṭabarānī, *Awsaṭ* (1059)[4]

1 There are five conditions for the acceptance of a person's testimony in an Islamic court: 1. Islam, 2. majority, 3. sanity, 4. freedom and 5. probity. The last condition of probity requires that a person avoids committing major sins and persistent commission of minor sins, and be a person of public decency according to the social norms of the time and place in which he lives.

A major sin is defined, as one for which there is a threat of severe punishment for its commission in the Qur'an or Sunnah. Examples of this are murder, adultery, and taking interest. A minor sin is whatever is less than this. So, committing a major sin once or persistently committing minor sins (to the extent that they outnumber acts of obedience) nullifies probity.

2 Ṭabarānī has Zayd ibn Thābit.

3 Ṭabarānī has recorded this hadith from Ibn ʿAmr in the reference above.

4 This hadith has also been related from Abū Saʿīd al-Khudrī by Ṭabarānī in *Awsaṭ* (4782), from Ibn ʿAbbās by Aḥmad (2968) and from Saʿd ibn ʿUbādah by Aḥmad (22460).

The Book of Virtues

٩٦ - حَدِيْثُ الْإِسْرَاء.

96. The hadith of the Nocturnal Journey.[1]

	Narrator	*Compiler(s)*
1	Anas	Būkhārī (3342) and Muslim (162)
2	Mālik ibn Ṣaʿṣaʿah	Būkhārī (3207) and Muslim (164)
3	Abū Dharr	Būkhārī (349) and Muslim (163)
4	Jābir ibn ʿAbdillāh	Būkhārī and Muslim (271)
5	Buraydah	Tirmidhī (3132)
6	Ḥudhayfah ibn al-Yamān	Tirmidhī[2]
7	Ibn ʿAbbās	Nasāʾī and Aḥmad (2324)
8	Ubayy ibn Kaʿb	*Zawāʾid al-Musnad*[3]
9	Abū Saʿīd al-Khudrī	Bayhaqī, *Dalāʾil*[4]
10	Shaddād ibn Aws	Bayhaqī, *Dalāʾil* (2:355)
11	Abū Hurayrah	Bayhaqī, *Dalāʾil* (2:357)
12	ʿĀʾishah	Bayhaqī, *Dalāʾil* (2:361)
13	Ibn Masʿūd	Ibn ʿArfah[5]
14	ʿAlī ibn Abī Ṭālib	Bazzār[6]
15	ʿUmar ibn al-Khaṭṭāb	Ibn Marduwayh[7]

1 See appendix for a variation of the hadith.
2 Ṭayālisī (411).
3 Aḥmad (21288).
4 Ḥārith ibn Abī Usāmah, *Baghiyyat al-Bāḥith* (27).
5 Bazzār (1568).
6 Shajarī al-Jurjānī, *Tartīb al-Amālī* (2:181).
7 Muttaqī al-Hindī (35838).

16	Abū Ḥabbah al-Anṣārī	Ibn Marduwayh[1]
17	Abū Ya'lā al-Anṣārī	Ibn Marduwayh
18	Abu 'l-Ḥamrā'	Ibn Marduwayh[2]
19	Abū Ayyūb	Ibn Marduwayh[3]
20	Abū Umāmah	Ibn Marduwayh[4]
21	Samurah ibn Jundub	Ibn Marduwayh[5]
22	Ibn 'Amr	Ibn Marduwayh[6]
23	Ṣuhayb	Ibn Marduwayh[7]
24	Asmā' bint Abī Bakr	Ibn Marduwayh
25	'Abd ar-Raḥmān ibn Qurṭ	Sa'īd ibn Manṣūr[8]
26	Umm Hāni'	Ṭabarānī, *Kabīr* (1059)
27	Umm Salamah	Ibn Sa'd (1:166)

٩٧ - اَلْجَمَلُ الَّذِي شَكَى إِلَيْهِ صَلَّى اللهُ عَلَيْهِ وَسَلَّمَ مَالِكَهُ.

97. The hadith of the camel that complained to the Prophet ﷺ about its owner.[9]

	Narrator	*Compiler(s)*
1	Anas	Aḥmad (12614)
2	Jarīr ibn 'Abdillāh	Dāraquṭnī

1 Aḥmad (21288).
2 Ṭabarānī, *Kabīr* (526).
3 Aḥmad (23552).
4 Ṭabarānī, *Kabīr* (7666).
5 Aḥmad (20101).
6 Muttaqī al-Hindī, *Kanz* (35044).
7 Ṭabarānī, *Kabīr* (7313).
8 Ṭabarānī, *Awsaṭ* (3742).
9 See appendix for a variation of the hadith.
This and the following hadith are two of many in which animals and inanimate objects are related to have spoken to the Prophet ﷺ. The scholars mention that the miracles of the Prophet ﷺ other than the Qur'an, despite their individual narrations not reaching the level of mass transmission, nevertheless indicate the general mass-transmitted truth that miracles appeared at the Prophet's hands ﷺ.

3	Yaʿlā ibn Murrah	Aḥmad (17548) and Ṭabarānī, *Aḥādīth Ṭiwāl* (54)
4	Abū Hurayrah	Bazzār (8023)
5	Jābir ibn ʿAbdillāh	Aḥmad (14332)
6	ʿAbdullāh ibn Masʿūd	Bazzār[1]
7	Yaʿlā ibn Umayyah	Ṭabarānī[2]

٩٨ - حَنِيْنُ الْجِذْعِ.

98. The hadith of the tree stump longing for the Prophet ﷺ.[3]

	Narrator	*Compiler(s)*
1	Sahl ibn Saʿd	Būkhārī (917) and Muslim (44)[4]
2	Jābir ibn ʿAbdillāh	Bukhārī (3584)
3	Ibn ʿUmar	Bukhārī (3583)
4	Ubayy Ibn Kaʿb	Dārimī (36)
5	Buraydah	Dārimī (32)
6	Kaʿb Ibn Mālik	Dārimī (36)
7	Abū Saʿīd al-Khudrī	Dārimī (37)
8	Anas	Tirmidhī (3627)
9	Umm Salamah	Bayhaqī, *Dalāʾil*[5]
10	Muṭṭallib ibn Abī Wadāʿah as-Sahmī	Bayhaqī, *Dalāʾil*[6]

1 Ṭabarānī, *Awsaṭ* (9189).

2 Haythamī, *Majmaʿ* (1416).

This hadith has also been related by Ibn ʿAbbās in Ṭabarānī, *Kabīr* (12003).

3 See appendix for a variation of the hadith.

4 In these references, Bukhārī and Muslim have recorded this incident of the construction of the pulpit but without the mention of the weeping tree stump.

5 Ṭabarānī, *Kabīr* (524).

6 ʿIrāqī, Ibn as-Subkī and Zubaydī in *Takhrīj Aḥādīth Iḥyāʾ* (3:1504).

This hadith is also related from ʿĀʾishah by Abū Nuʿaym in *Dalāʾil* (310).

٩٩ - أُعْطِيتُ خَمْسًا لَمْ يُعْطَهُنَّ أَحَدٌ مِنْ الأَنْبِيَاءِ قَبْلِي.

99. 'I was given five things that no prophet before me was given. . .'[1]

	Narrator	Compiler(s)
1	Jābir ibn ʿAbdillāh	Būkhārī (335) and Muslim (521)
2	Abū Hurayrah	Būkhārī and Muslim (523)[2]
3	ʿAlī	Aḥmad (763)
4	Ibn ʿAbbās	Aḥmad (2256)
5	Ibn ʿAmr	Aḥmad (7068)
6	Abū Dharr	Aḥmad (21314)
7	Abū Mūsā	Aḥmad (1973)
8	Ibn ʿUmar	Ṭabarānī, *Kabīr* (13522)
9	Sā'ib ibn Yazīd	Ṭabarānī, *Kabīr* (6674)
10	Abū Saʿīd	Ṭabarānī, *Awsaṭ* (7439)

١٠٠ - لَا نُورَثُ، مَا تَرَكْنَاهُ صَدَقَةٌ.

100. 'We [i.e. prophets] do not leave inheritance; whatever we leave behind is charity.'

	Narrator	Compiler(s)
1	ʿUmar	Būkhārī (3094) and Muslim (49)
2	ʿUthmān	Būkhārī (3094) and Muslim (49)
3	ʿAlī	Būkhārī (3094) and Muslim (49)
4	Saʿd ibn Abī Waqqāṣ	Būkhārī (3094) and Muslim (49)
5	ʿAbbās	Būkhārī (3094) and Muslim (49)[3]

1 See appendix for a variation of the hadith.

2 The hadith quoted by Muslim lists six things.

3 Hadiths (3094) in Bukhārī and (49) in Muslim are related by Mālik ibn Aws, who relates these words from ʿUmar. Mālik was sitting in the company of ʿUmar when ʿUthmān, ʿAbd ar-Raḥmān ibn ʿAwf, Zubayr and Saʿd joined them, followed by ʿAlī and ʿAbbās. ʿUmar related these words and asked those present if they had heard them too and they responded in the affirmative.

6	Abū Bakr aṣ-Ṣiddīq	Muslim (52)
7	ʿAbd ar-Raḥmān ibn ʿAwf	Muslim (49)
8	Zubayr ibn al-ʿAwwām	Muslim (49)
9	Abū Hurayrah	Muslim (1760)
10	ʿĀʾishah	Abū Dāwūd (2968)
11	Ṭalḥah	Nasāʾī, *As-Sunan al-Kubrā* (6275)
12	Ḥudhayfah	Ṭabarānī, *Awsaṭ* (1806)
13	Ibn ʿAbbās	Ṭabarānī, *Awsaṭ* (4933)

Eight of the ten who were guaranteed Paradise have related this, like the hadith: 'Whoever lies about me. . .'

١٠١ - لَوْ كُنْتُ مُتَّخِذًا خَلِيلًا لَاتَّخَذْتُ أَبَا بَكْرٍ خَلِيلًا.

101. 'If I were to have had a bosom friend, it would have been Abū Bakr.'

	Narrator	*Compiler(s)*
1	Abū Saʿīd	Būkhārī (466) and Muslim (2382)
2	Ibn ʿAbbās	Būkhārī (467) and Muslim
3	Ibn az-Zubayr	Bukhārī (3658)
4	Ibn Masʿūd	Muslim (2383)
5	Jundub al-Bajalī	Muslim (532)
6	Abu 'l-Muʿallā	Tirmidhī (3659)
7	Abū Hurayrah	Tirmidhī (3661)
8	Anas	Bazzār (6557)
9	Ibn ʿUmar	Ṭabarānī, *Kabīr* (13383)
10	Ibn ʿAbbās	Ṭabarānī, *Kabīr* (11938)
11	Abū Wāqid	Ṭabarānī, *Kabīr* (3297)
12	ʿĀʾishah	Ṭabarānī, *Awsaṭ* (2055)

١٠٢ - مَنْ كُنْتُ مَوْلَاهُ فَعَلِيٌّ مَوْلَاهُ.

102. 'Whoever I was the master of, ʿAlī is his master.'

	Narrator	*Compiler(s)*
1	Ibn Arqam	Tirmidhī (3713)
2	ʿAlī	Aḥmad (641)
3	Abū Ayyūb al-Anṣārī	Aḥmad (23563)
4	ʿUmar	Bazzār[1]
5	Dhū Marr[2]	Bazzār (786)
6	Abū Hurayrah	Bazzār (9655)
7	Ṭalḥah	Bazzār[3]
8	Umārah	Bazzār[4]
9	Ibn ʿAbbās	Bazzār (4352)
10	Buraydah	Bazzār (4352)
11	Ibn ʿUmar	Ṭabarānī, *Kabīr* (13876)
12	Mālik ibn al-Ḥuwayrith	Ṭabarānī, *Kabīr* (646)
13	Ḥabshah ibn Junādah[5]	Ṭabarānī, *Kabīr* (3514)
14	Jarīr	Ṭabarānī, *Kabīr* (2505)
15	Saʿd ibn Abī Waqqāṣ	Ṭabarānī[6]
16	Abū Saʿīd al-Khudrī	Ṭabarānī, *Awsaṭ* (8434)
17	Anas	Ṭabarānī, *Ṣaghīr* (175)
18	Jundaʿ al-Anṣārī	Abū Nuʿaym[7]
19	ʿUmar ibn ʿAbd al-ʿAzīz from a number of Companions	Ibn ʿAsākir (2177)
20	Qays ibn Thābit	Ibn ʿAqdah[8]

1 Dhahabī, *Risālah Ṭuruq Ḥadīth Man Kuntu Mawlāhu* (105).

2 Or Dhū Murr.

3 Ḥākim (5594).

4 I have not found this hadith. However, Dhahabī in *Risālah* records this hadith from Umārah, who relates from Abū Mijlaz and he relates from ʿAlī (111).

5 Ṭabarānī has Ḥabashī.

6 Aḥmad, *Faḍāʾil aṣ-Ṣaḥābah* (1093).

7 Ibn Kathīr, *Jāmiʿ al-Masānīd* (2:239).

8 Zaylaʿī, *Takhrīj Aḥādīth al-Kashshāf* (2:240).

21	Ḥabīb ibn Budayl ibn Warqā'	Ibn ʿAqdah[1]
22	Yazīd (or Zayd) ibn Shurāḥbīl al-Anṣārī	Yaʿlā ibn Murrah

Ibn ʿAsākir has quoted ʿUmar ibn ʿAbd al-ʿAzīz as saying, 'A number of Companions of the Prophet ﷺ told me that they heard the Messenger of Allah ﷺ say this. . .' Ibn ʿAqdah has quoted in his book Muwālāh Zirr ibn Ḥubaysh as saying, "ʿAlī ؓ said, "Who here is from the Companions of the Prophet?" Twelve men stood up, among whom were Qays ibn Thābit and Ḥabīb ibn Budayl ibn Warqā', and they all testified that they had heard the Messenger of Allah ﷺ say this. . .' He has also quoted Yaʿlā ibn Murrah as saying, 'When ʿAlī came to Kufah, he implored the people, "Who has heard the Messenger of Allah ﷺ say..?" and ten or so men verified that for him.'

١٠٣ - أَمَا تَرْضَى أَنْ تَكُونَ مِنِّي بِمَنْزِلَةِ هَارُونَ مِنْ مُوسَى.

103. 'Are you [ʿAlī] not pleased that you are to me as Hārūn was to Mūsā?'

	Narrator	*Compiler(s)*
1	Abū Saʿīd al-Khudrī	Aḥmad (11272)
2	Asmā' bint ʿUmais	Aḥmad (27081)
4	Umm Salamah	Ṭabarānī, *Kabīr* (12341)
5	Ḥubaysh ibn Junādah[2]	Ṭabarānī, *Awsaṭ* (7592)
6	Ibn ʿUmar	Ṭabarānī, *Awsaṭ* (1465)
7	ʿAlī	Ṭabarānī, *Awsaṭ* (4248)
8	Jābir ibn Samurah	Ṭabarānī, *Kabīr* (2035)
9	Barā' ibn ʿĀzib	Ṭabarānī, *Kabīr* (5095)
10	Zayd ibn Arqam	Ṭabarānī, *Kabīr* (5094)

1 Ibn Kathīr, *Jāmiʿ al-Masānīd* (2:297).

2 Ṭabarānī has Ḥabashī ibn Junādah.

١٠٤ - تَقْتُلُ عَمَّارَ الْفِئَةُ الْبَاغِيَةُ.

104. "ʿAmmār shall be killed by the unjust faction."[1]

	Narrator	Compiler(s)
1	Abū Saʿīd	Būkhārī (447) and Muslim (2915)
2	Abū Qatādah	Muslim[2]
3	Umm Salamah	Muslim (2916)
4	Ḥudhayfah	Ḥākim (5676)
5	Ibn Masʿūd[3]	Ḥākim (5676)
6	ʿAmmār ibn Yāsir	Aḥmad[4]
7	ʿAmr ibn al-ʿĀṣ	Aḥmad (17766)
8	Ibn ʿAbdillāh	Aḥmad[5]
9	ʿAmr ibn Ḥazm	Aḥmad (42)
10	Khuzaymah ibn Thābit	Aḥmad (21873)
11	ʿUthmān	Abū Yaʿlā, *Muʿjam* (283); and Ṭabarānī, *Ṣaghīr* (516)
12	Anas	Abū Yaʿlā and Ṭabarānī, *Awsaṭ* (6315)
13	Abū Hurayrah	Abū Yaʿlā (6524) and Ṭabarānī
14	Abū Rāfiʿ	Rāfiʿī, *Tārīkh*[6]
15	Jābir ibn ʿAbdillāh	Ibn ʿAsākir (42:224)

---

1 Imam Muslim's ‎ collection of authentic hadith alone has five different chains for this hadith. Imam Nawawī comments:

The scholars say that this hadith is an obvious proof that ʿAlī was right and correct, and the other faction erred; however, they were *mujtahids*, so there is no sin upon them, as we mentioned previously in several places, including this chapter. There is an obvious miracle of Allah's Messenger in the hadith from a number of perspectives. Among them is [predicting] that ʿAmmār's death would be from killing, that Muslims would kill him, that they were in the wrong, that the Companions would fight one another and that they would be two factions, one in the wrong and the other not so. All of this happened in a manner as clear as the rising of the dawn. May Allah bless and give peace to His Messenger, who does not speak from whim; rather, it is but revelation revealed!

2 Aḥmad (22610).

3 Ḥākim records the hadith from Abū Masʿūd.

4 Ṭayālisī (684).

5 I could not find this hadith from this narrator. Bazzār (2948), however, has quoted Muslim al-Aʿwar – also knows as Ibn ʿAbdillāh, who relates from Ḥabbah that Ḥudhayfah and Abū Masʿūd discussed this. One of them mentioned it and the other confirmed it.

6 Ṭabarānī, *Kabīr* (954).

He [i.e. Ibn ʿAsākir] said, 'It has been related in the hadiths of ʿAmmār, ʿUthmān ibn ʿAffān, Muʿāwiyah ibn Abī Sufyān, ʿAbdullāh ibn ʿAbbās, ʿAmr ibn al-ʿĀṣ, his son ʿAbdullāh, Ibn ʿUmar, Abū Rāfiʿ, Abdullāh ibn Masʿūd, Ḥudhayfah ibn al-Yamān, Abū Hurayrah, Abū Saʿīd, Zayd ibn Abī Awfā al-Aslamī, Jābir ibn Samurah, Jābir ibn ʿAbdillāh, Abū Qatādah, ʿAmr ibn Ḥazam, Khuzaymah ibn Thābit, Abu 'l-Yusr, Kaʿb ibn ʿAmr, Ziyād ibn al-Fard, Kaʿb ibn Mālik, Anas, Abū Umāmah al-Bāhilī, ʿĀ'ishah and Umm Salamah,' and then he mentioned all of their chains of narration.

١٠٥ - الْحَسَنُ وَالْحُسَيْنُ سَيِّدَا شَبَابِ أَهْلِ الْجَنَّةِ.

105. 'Ḥasan and Ḥusayn will be the leaders of the youth of Paradise.'

	Narrator	*Compiler(s)*
1	Abū Saʿīd	Aḥmad (10999) and Tirmidhī (3768)
2	Ḥudhayfah ibn al-Yamān	Tirmidhī (3781)
3	ʿUmar ibn al-Khaṭṭāb	Ṭabarānī, *Kabīr* (2598)
4	ʿAlī	Ṭabarānī, *Kabīr* (2599)
5	Jābir ibn ʿAbdillāh	Ṭabarānī, *Kabīr* (2616)
6	Ḥusayn ibn ʿAlī	Ṭabarānī, *Awsaṭ* (366)
7	Usāmah Ibn Zayd	Ṭabarānī, *Awsaṭ* (5208)
8	Barā' Ibn ʿĀzib	Ṭabarānī, *Awsaṭ* (4332)
9	Qurrah ibn Iyās	Ṭabarānī, *Kabīr* (2617)
10	Mālik ibn al-Ḥuwayrith	Ṭabarānī, *Kabīr* (650)
11	Abū Hurayrah	Ṭabarānī, *Kabīr* (2604)
12	Ibn ʿUmar	Ibn ʿAdī[1]
13	Ibn Masʿūd	Ibn ʿAdī[2]
14	Anas	Ibn ʿAdī[3]

1 Ibn Mājah (118).

2 Muttaqī al-Hindī, *Kanz* (34346).

3 Ibn ʿAsākir (13:211).

15	Buraydah	Ibn ʿAsākir (13:210)
16	Ibn ʿAbbās	Ibn ʿAsākir (11:132)

١٠٦ - اهْتَزَّ الْعَرْشُ لِمَوْتِ سَعْدِ بْنِ مُعَاذٍ.

106. 'The Throne shook at the death of Saʿd ibn Muʿādh.'

	Narrator	*Compiler(s)*
1	Jābir	Būkhārī (3803), Muslim (2466) and Ahmad
2	Anas	Muslim (2467) and Aḥmad
3	Usayd ibn Huḍayr	Ḥākim (4927)
4	Ibn ʿUmar	Aḥmad and Bazzār (5737)
5	Muʿayqīb	Ṭabarānī, *Kabīr* (5341)
6	Abū Saʿīd	Aḥmad (11184) and Abū Yaʿlā (1260)

١٠٧ - أَنَّه سَمِعَ قِرَاءَةَ أَبِي مُوسَى اَلْأَشْعَرِي فَقَالَ : لَقَدْ أُوتِيَ مِزْمَارًا مِنْ مَزَامِيرِ آلِ دَاوُدَ.

107. The Prophet ﷺ heard Abū Mūsā al-Ashʿarī's recitation of the Qur'an and said, 'Verily, he has been given a flute from the flutes of the family of Dāwūd.'

	Narrator	*Compiler(s)*
1	Buraydah[1]	Būkhārī (5048) and Muslim (236)
2	Abū Hurayrah	Aḥmad (8646), Nasā'ī (1019) and Ibn Mājah (1341)
3	ʿĀ'ishah	Nasā'ī (1021)
4	Anas	Abū Yaʿlā[2]
5	Salamah ibn Qays	Bazzār and Ṭabarānī, *Kabīr* (6318)

1 Both Bukhārī and Muslim have Abū Burdah.

2 Abū Nuʿaym, *Ḥilyah* (1:258).

6	ʿAbd ar-Raḥmān ibn Kaʿb ibn Mālik (NCM)	Bazzār and Ṭabarānī, *Kabīr* (161)

١٠٨ - خَيْرُ النَّاسِ قَرْنِي ثُمَّ الَّذِينَ يَلُونَهُمْ ثُمَّ الَّذِينَ يَلُونَهُمْ.

108. 'The best people are those of my century, then those who follow them, then those who follow them.'

	Narrator	*Compiler(s)*
1	Ibn Masʿūd	Būkhārī (2652) and Muslim (2533)
2	ʿImrān ibn Ḥuṣayn	Būkhārī (2651) and Muslim (2535)
3	Abū Hurayrah	Muslim (2534) and Aḥmad (9318)
4	ʿĀ'ishah	Muslim (2536) and Aḥmad (25233)
7	Buraydah	Aḥmad (22960)
8	Nuʿmān ibn Bashīr	Aḥmad (18428)
9	ʿUmar	Ṭayālisī (297)
10	Saʿd ibn Tamīm	Ṭabarānī, *Kabīr* (5460)
11	Jamīlah bint Abī Lahab[1]	Ṭabarānī, *Kabīr* (540)
12	ʿAmr ibn Shuraḥbīl (NCM)	Ibn Abī Shaybah (32416)

1 Ṭabarānī has Bint Abī Jahl.

The Book of the Resurrection

١٠٩ - سُؤالُ الْمَيِّتِ فِي قَبْرِهِ.

109. The hadith of the questioning of the deceased in his grave.[1]

	Narrator	*Compiler(s)*
1	Anas	Būkhārī (1338) and Muslim (2870)
2	Asmā' bint Abī Bakr	Būkhārī (1373)
3	ʿAmr ibn al-ʿĀṣ	Muslim[2]
4	Barā' Ibn ʿĀzib	Abū Dāwūd (4753)
5	ʿUthmān	Abū Dāwūd (3221)
6	Abū Hurayrah	Tirmidhī (1071), Ḥākim and Ibn Mājah (4268)

١١٠ - حَدِيْثُ الْحَوْضِ.

110. The hadith of the Basin.[3]

	Narrator	*Compiler(s)*
1	Anas	Būkhārī (6582) and Muslim (1059)
2	Usayd ibn Ḥuḍayr	Būkhārī (3792) and Muslim (1845)
3	Jundub ibn ʿAbdillāh ibn Sufyān al-Bajalī	Būkhārī (6589)
4	Ḥārithah ibn Wahb	Būkhārī (6591) and Muslim (2298)

1 See appendix for a variation of the hadith.
2 Ibn Ḥibbān, *Mawārid az-Ẓam'ān* (778).
3 See appendix for a variation of the hadith.

5	Sahl ibn Saʿd	Būkhārī (6583) and Muslim (2290)
6	ʿAbdullāh ibn Zayd	Būkhārī and Muslim (1061)
7	Ibn ʿUmar	Būkhārī (6577) and Muslim (2299)
8	Ibn ʿAmr	Būkhārī (6579) and Muslim (2292)
9	Ibn Masʿūd	Būkhārī (6575) and Muslim (2297)
10	Mustawrid ibn Shaddād	Būkhārī and Muslim[1]
11	Abū Hurayrah	Būkhārī (6585) and Muslim (247)
12	Asmā' bint Abī Bakr	Būkhārī (6593) and Muslim (2292)
13	Ibn ʿAbbās	Būkhārī (6578)
14	Thawbān	Muslim (2301)
15	Jābir ibn Samurah	Muslim (2305)
16	Ḥudhayfah ibn al-Yamān	Muslim (2297)
17	ʿUqbah ibn ʿĀmir	Muslim (2296)
18	Abū Dharr	Muslim (2300)
19	Abū Saʿīd	Muslim (2290)
20	ʿĀ'ishah	Muslim (2294)
21	Umm Salamah	Muslim (2295)
22	Abū Bakr aṣ-Ṣiddīq	Abū Awānah (443)
23	ʿUmar ibn al-Khaṭṭāb	Bayhaqī, *Shuʿab* (10003)
24	ʿUtbah ibn ʿAbd as-Sulamī	Bayhaqī, *Shuʿab*[2]
25	ʿAlī ibn Abī Ṭālib	Abū Nuʿaym, *Ḥilyah* (9:64)
26	Samurah ibn Jundub	Tirmidhī[3]
27	Usāmah ibn Zayd	Ḥākim (4886)
28	Ḥamzah ibn ʿAbd al-Muṭṭalib	Ḥākim[4]
29	Khawlah bint Qays	Ḥākim[5]
30	Khabbāb ibn al-Aratt	Ḥākim (262)
31	Zayd ibn Arqam	Ḥākim (256)

1 Ṭabarānī has recorded a hadith in *Kabīr* about the Basin from Ḥārithah ibn Wahb and Mustawrid added, 'Its cups are like the stars' (3262).

2 Bayhaqī, *Baʿth* (274).

3 Ṭabarānī, *Kabīr* (7053).

4 I could not find this hadith related from Ḥamzah but there is mention of him in the hadith of the Basin related from his wife Khawlah by Aḥmad (27316).

5 Aḥmad (27316). Aḥmad also has a similar narration related by Khawlah bint Ḥakīm (27315).

32	ʿĀʾidh ibn ʿAmr	Ḥākim[1]
33	Kaʿb ibn ʿUjrah	Ḥākim (263)
34	Laqīṭ ibn ʿĀmir	Ḥākim[2]
35	Abū Barzah	Ḥākim (255)
36	Buraydah	Bazzār (4381)
37	Ubayy ibn Kaʿb	Ṭabarānī[3]
38	Barāʾ ibn ʿĀzib	Ṭabarānī, *Awsaṭ* (3384)
39	Jābir ibn ʿAbdillāh	Ṭabarānī, *Awsaṭ* (749)
40	Ḥudhayfah ibn Asīd[4]	Ṭabarānī, *Kabīr* (2683)
41	Ḥasan ibn ʿAlī	Ṭabarānī, *Awsaṭ* (2405)
42	Zayd ibn Thābit	Ṭabarānī, *Kabīr* (4921)
43	Salmān	Ṭabarānī[5]
44	Abū Umāmah	Ṭabarānī, *Kabīr* (7632)
45	Abū Bakrah	Ṭabarānī, *Musnad as-Shāmiyyīn* (2660)
46	Abu ad-Dardāʾ	Ṭabarānī, *Awsaṭ* (397)
47	Abū Masʿūd	Ṭabarānī, *Kabīr* (538)
48	Suwayd ibn Jabalah al-Fazārī	Abū Zurʿah, *Musnad ash-Shāmiyyīn*[6]
49	ʿIrbāḍ ibn Sāriyah	Ibn Ḥibbān (7239)
50	Nawwās ibn Samʿān	Ibn Abī ad-Dunyā[7]

١١١ - يَدْخُلُ الْجَنَّةَ سَبْعُونَ أَلْفًا بِغَيْرِ حِسَابٍ.

111. 'Seventy thousand will enter Paradise without any reckoning.'

	Narrator	*Compiler(s)*
1	Ibn ʿAbbās	Bukhārī (5752) and Muslim (220)

1 Bazzār (2435).
2 Aḥmad (16206).
3 Ibn Abī ʿĀṣim, *Sunnah* (717).
4 Or Usayd.
5 Ḥākim (4662).
6 Ṭabarānī, *Musnad ash-Shāmiyyīn* (1849).
7 Ibn Bashkwāl, *Dhayl ʿalā Juzʾ Baqī ibn Makhlad* (84).

2	Abū Hurayrah	Būkhārī (6542)[1] and Muslim (216)
3	ʿImrān ibn Ḥuṣayn	Muslim (218)
4	Abū Umāmah	Tirmidhī (2437)
5	Abū Bakr aṣ-Ṣiddīq	Aḥmad (22)
6	ʿAbd ar-Raḥmān ibn Abī Bakr	Aḥmad (1706)
7	Ibn Masʿūd	Aḥmad (3819)
8	Jābir ibn ʿAbdillāh	Aḥmad (14721)
9	Abū Ayyūb al-Anṣārī	Aḥmad (23505)
10	Thawbān	Aḥmad (22418)
11	Ḥudhayfah ibn al-Yamān	Aḥmad (23336)
12	Anas	Bazzār (6398)
13	Abū Saʿīd al-Khudrī	Bazzār
14	Rifāʿah al-Juhanī	Bazzār[2]
15	Falatān ibn ʿĀṣim	Bazzār (3700)
16	Samurah ibn Jundub	Bazzār (4672)
17	ʿAmr ibn Ḥazm	Ṭabarānī[3]
18	Abū Saʿīd al-Anṣārī	Ṭabarānī, *Kabīr* (771)
19	Asmāʾ bint Abī Bakr	Ṭabarānī, *Kabīr* (240)[4]

١١٢ - حَدِيْثُ الشَّفَاعَةِ.

112. The long hadith of the Intercession and people's seeking it from one prophet to another.[5]

	Narrator	*Compiler(s)*
1	Anas	Būkhārī (4476) and Muslim (193)
2	Abū Hurayrah	Būkhārī (4712) and Muslim (194)
3	Ibn ʿUmar	Būkhārī (4718) and Muslim

1 Bukhārī quotes this very hadith from Abū Hurayrah but without the words 'without any reckoning.'

2 Ibn Khuzaymah, *Tawḥīd* (37).

3 Bayhaqī, *Shuʿab* (264).

4 This hadith has also been related by Khabbāb (Bazzār 2120).

5 See appendix for a variation of the hadith.

4	Ḥudhayfah	Muslim[1]
5	Jābir	Muslim (191)
6	Abū Bakr	Aḥmad (15)
7	Ibn ʿAbbās	Aḥmad (2546)
8	Ubayy Ibn Kaʿb	Aḥmad (21245)
9	Abū Saʿīd	Tirmidhī (3418)
10	Salmān	Ṭabarānī, *Kabīr* (6117)
11	ʿUqbah Ibn ʿĀmir	Ṭabarānī, *Kabīr* (887)
12	ʿUbādah Ibn aṣ-Ṣāmit	Ḥākim (82)

١١٣ - بُعِثْتُ أَنَا وَالسَّاعَةَ كَهَاتَيْنِ.

113. 'I was sent before the Hour like this.'[2]

	Narrator	*Compiler(s)*
1	Anas	Būkhārī (6504) and Muslim (2951)
2	Sahl ibn Saʿd	Būkhārī (4936) and Muslim (2950)
3	Abū Hurayrah	Būkhārī (6505)
4	Mustawrid ibn Shaddād	Tirmidhī (2213)
5	Buraydah	Aḥmad (22947)
6	Jābir ibn Samurah	Aḥmad (20981)
7	Wahb ibn as-Suwāʾī	Aḥmad (18770)
8	Ibn ʿUmar	Aḥmad (5115)[3]
9	Abū Jubayrah ibn aḍ-Ḍaḥḥāk	Ṭabarānī, *Kabīr* (971)
10	From elders of the Anṣār	Bazzār[4]

1 Ibn Abī Shaybah (31744).

2 The Prophet ﷺ held his index and middle fingers together.

3 This variation has '*bayna yadayi 's-sāʿah*,' (just before the Hour) instead of '*kahātayn*,' (like this).

4 I could not find this hadith from elders of the Anṣār in Bazzār. It is possible that this is an error in the transcription, since Abū Jubayrah (the previous narrator) relates many of his hadith from 'elders of the Anṣār.' Therefore, narrators 9 and 10 would be understood to be from one chain. See Ṭabarānī, *Kabīr* (972); Ibn al-Mubārak (1592); and Ibn Abī Shaybah, *Musnad* (948), for the same hadith where Abū Jubayrah relates from elders of the Anṣār.

Appendix

8. THE HADITH OF JIBRĪL

بَيْنَمَا نَحْنُ عِنْدَ رَسُولِ اللهِ صَلَّى اللهُ عَلَيْهِ وَسَلَّمَ ذَاتَ يَوْمٍ، إِذْ طَلَعَ عَلَيْنَا رَجُلٌ شَدِيدُ بَيَاضِ الثِّيَابِ شَدِيدُ سَوَادِ الشَّعْرِ لَا يُرَى عَلَيْهِ أَثَرُ السَّفَرِ وَلَا يَعْرِفُهُ مِنَّا أَحَدٌ، حَتَّى جَلَسَ إِلَى النَّبِيِّ صَلَّى اللهُ عَلَيْهِ وَسَلَّمَ فَأَسْنَدَ رُكْبَتَيْهِ إِلَى رُكْبَتَيْهِ وَوَضَعَ كَفَّيْهِ عَلَى فَخِذَيْهِ وَقَالَ: يَا مُحَمَّدُ أَخْبِرْنِي عَنِ الْإِسْلَامِ. فَقَالَ رَسُولُ اللهِ صَلَّى اللهُ عَلَيْهِ وَسَلَّمَ: الْإِسْلَامُ أَنْ تَشْهَدَ أَنْ لَا إِلَهَ إِلَّا اللهُ وَأَنَّ مُحَمَّدًا رَسُولُ اللهِ، وَتُقِيمَ الصَّلَاةَ، وَتُؤْتِيَ الزَّكَاةَ، وَتَصُومَ رَمَضَانَ، وَتَحُجَّ الْبَيْتَ إِنِ اسْتَطَعْتَ إِلَيْهِ سَبِيلًا. قَالَ: صَدَقْتَ، قَالَ: فَعَجِبْنَا لَهُ يَسْأَلُهُ وَيُصَدِّقُهُ. قَالَ: فَأَخْبِرْنِي عَنِ الْإِيمَانِ. قَالَ: أَنْ تُؤْمِنَ بِاللهِ، وَمَلَائِكَتِهِ، وَكُتُبِهِ، وَرُسُلِهِ، وَالْيَوْمِ الْآخِرِ، وَتُؤْمِنَ بِالْقَدَرِ خَيْرِهِ وَشَرِّهِ. قَالَ: صَدَقْتَ. قَالَ: فَأَخْبِرْنِي عَنِ الْإِحْسَانِ. قَالَ: أَنْ تَعْبُدَ اللهَ كَأَنَّكَ تَرَاهُ، فَإِنْ لَمْ تَكُنْ تَرَاهُ فَإِنَّهُ يَرَاكَ. قَالَ: فَأَخْبِرْنِي عَنِ السَّاعَةِ. قَالَ: مَا الْمَسْئُولُ عَنْهَا بِأَعْلَمَ مِنَ السَّائِلِ. قَالَ: فَأَخْبِرْنِي عَنْ أَمَارَتِهَا. قَالَ: أَنْ تَلِدَ الْأَمَةُ رَبَّتَهَا، وَأَنْ تَرَى الْحُفَاةَ الْعُرَاةَ الْعَالَةَ رِعَاءَ الشَّاءِ يَتَطَاوَلُونَ فِي الْبُنْيَانِ. ثُمَّ انْطَلَقَ فَلَبِثْتُ مَلِيًّا ثُمَّ قَالَ لِي: يَا عُمَرُ، أَتَدْرِي مَنِ السَّائِلُ؟ قُلْتُ: اللهُ وَرَسُولُهُ أَعْلَمُ. قَالَ: هَذَا جِبْرِيلُ أَتَاكُمْ يُعَلِّمُكُمْ دِينَكُمْ.

[On the authority of ʿUmar ﷺ:]

One day we were with Allah's Messenger ﷺ when a man with extremely white clothes and extremely black hair with no sign of having travelled came to us, and no one knew who he was. He sat before the Prophet ﷺ, putting his knees to the Prophet's knees and placing his hands on the Prophet's thighs. He said, 'O Muḥammad! Tell me about Islam.' So Allah's Messenger ﷺ said, 'Islam is that you testify that there is no god but Allah and that Muḥammad is Allah's Messenger, establish prayer, pay zakat, fast Ramaḍān and make Pilgrimage to the House if you are able to find a way.' He said, 'You have told the truth,' and we were amazed at him for asking him then affirming! He said, 'Tell me about faith.' The Prophet said, 'That you believe in Allah, His angels, His books, His Messengers, the Last Day and predetermination—the good and the bad.' He said, 'You have told the truth. Tell me about *iḥsān*.' He said, 'That you worship Allah as if you see him; and if you do not see him, then know that He sees you.' He said, 'Tell me about the Hour.' He said, 'The questioned has no more knowledgeable of it than the questioner.' He said, 'Then tell me about its signs.' He said, 'That the slave woman gives birth to her master, and that you see barefooted, naked and poor shepherds compete in building tall structures.' Then the man left. I wondered about this a long time until the Prophet said to me, 'O ʿUmar! Do you know who the questioner was?' I said, 'Allah and His Messenger know best.' He said, 'He was Jibrīl. He came to teach you your religion.'

12. WIPING OVER LEATHER SOCKS

عَنْ النَّبِيِّ صَلَّى اللهُ عَلَيْهِ وَسَلَّمَ أَنَّهُ مَسَحَ عَلَى الْخُفَّيْنِ.

The Prophet ﷺ wiped over his leather socks.

23. THE HADITH ON THE PRAYER TIMES

أَمَّنِي جِبْرِيلُ عَلَيْهِ السَّلَام عِنْدَ الْبَيْتِ مَرَّتَيْنِ، فَصَلَّى الظُّهْرَ فِي الْأُولَى مِنْهُمَا حِينَ كَانَ الْفَيْءُ مِثْلَ الشِّرَاكِ، ثُمَّ صَلَّى الْعَصْرَ حِينَ كَانَ كُلُّ شَيْءٍ مِثْلَ ظِلِّهِ، ثُمَّ صَلَّى الْمَغْرِبَ حِينَ وَجَبَتْ الشَّمْسُ وَأَفْطَرَ الصَّائِمُ، ثُمَّ صَلَّى الْعِشَاءَ حِينَ غَابَ الشَّفَقُ، ثُمَّ صَلَّى الْفَجْرَ حِينَ بَرَقَ الْفَجْرُ وَحَرُمَ الطَّعَامُ عَلَى الصَّائِمِ. وَصَلَّى الْمَرَّةَ الثَّانِيَةَ الظُّهْرَ حِينَ كَانَ ظِلُّ كُلِّ شَيْءٍ مِثْلَهُ لِوَقْتِ الْعَصْرِ بِالْأَمْسِ، ثُمَّ صَلَّى الْعَصْرَ حِينَ كَانَ ظِلُّ كُلِّ شَيْءٍ مِثْلَيْهِ، ثُمَّ صَلَّى الْمَغْرِبَ لِوَقْتِهِ الْأَوَّلِ، ثُمَّ صَلَّى الْعِشَاءَ الْآخِرَةَ حِينَ ذَهَبَ ثُلُثُ اللَّيْلِ، ثُمَّ صَلَّى الصُّبْحَ حِينَ أَسْفَرَتْ الْأَرْضُ. ثُمَّ الْتَفَتَ إِلَيَّ جِبْرِيلُ فَقَالَ: يَا مُحَمَّدُ هَذَا وَقْتُ الْأَنْبِيَاءِ مِنْ قَبْلِكَ وَالْوَقْتُ فِيمَا بَيْنَ هَذَيْنِ الْوَقْتَيْنِ.

[On the authority of Ibn ʿAbbās ﵄:] Allah's Messenger ﷺ said:

Jibrīl led me in prayer at the *Kaʿbah* twice. He prayed the midday prayer with me when the sun passed its zenith the amount of a sandal strap, the afternoon prayer when the length of his shadow was like him, the sunset prayer when the sun went down and the fasting person broke his fast, the night prayer when the sun disappeared from the horizon and the dawn prayer when dawn broke and food and drink were prohibited from the fasting person. The next day he prayed the midday prayer with me when the length of his shadow was like him, the afternoon prayer when the length of his shadow was twice his length, the sunset prayer at the same time as the first, the night prayer when the first third of the night passed and the dawn prayer when the Earth was bright. Then he turned to me and said, 'O Muḥammad, this is the time of the prophets before you, and the time is between these two times.'

26. THE PROPHET ﷺ SLEPT PAST THE DAWN PRAYER IN THE VALLEY [OF AL-QURĀ]

كَانَ رَسُولُ اللهِ صَلَّى اللهُ عَلَيْهِ وَآلِهِ وَسَلَّمَ فِي مَسِيرٍ لَهُ فَنَامُوا عَنْ صَلَاةِ الْفَجْرِ فَاسْتَيْقَظُوا بِحَرِّ الشَّمْسِ، فَارْتَفَعُوا قَلِيلًا حَتَّى اسْتَعْلَتْ ثُمَّ أَمَرَ الْمُؤَذِّنَ فَأَذَّنَ، ثُمَّ صَلَّى الرَّكْعَتَيْنِ قَبْلَ الْفَجْرِ، ثُمَّ أَقَامَ الْمُؤَذِّنُ فَصَلَّى الْفَجْرَ.

The Messenger of Allah ﷺ was on one of his journeys when the party slept past the dawn prayer and woke in the heat of the sun. They ascended a little until the sun had risen. Then he ﷺ gave the order to the muezzin, who gave the call to prayer. He prayed to units of prayer before the dawn prayer, then the muezzin gave the second call indicating the start of prayer (*iqāmah*) and he ﷺ prayed the dawn prayer.

32. RECITING THE BASMALAH OUT LOUD

كَانَ رَسُولُ اللهِ صَلَّى اللهُ عَلَيْهِ وَسَلَّمَ يَجْهَرُ بِبِسْمِ اللهِ الرَّحْمَنِ الرَّحِيمِ.

The Messenger of Allah ﷺ would recite, 'In the Name of Allah, the All-Merciful, the Most Merciful,' aloud.

33. Lifting the hands when opening the prayer, when bowing, and when straightening back up.

كَانَ إِذَا دَخَلَ فِي الصَّلَاةِ كَبَّرَ وَرَفَعَ يَدَيْهِ، وَإِذَا رَكَعَ رَفَعَ يَدَيْهِ، وَإِذَا قَالَ سَمِعَ اللهُ لِمَنْ حَمِدَهُ رَفَعَ يَدَيْهِ، وَإِذَا قَامَ مِنَ الرَّكْعَتَيْنِ رَفَعَ يَدَيْهِ.

When he ﷺ entered the prayer he said, '*Allāhu Akbar*,' and raised his hands; when he bowed he raised his hands; when he said, '*Samiʿa'llāhu li-man ḥamidah*,' he raised his hands; and when he stood back up after two units he raised his hands.

34. RECITING THE *TASHAHHUD*

كُنَّا نَقُولُ فِي الصَّلَاةِ خَلْفَ رَسُولِ اللهِ صَلَّى اللهُ عَلَيْهِ وَسَلَّمَ: السَّلَامُ عَلَى اللهِ السَّلَامُ عَلَى فُلَانٍ. فَقَالَ لَنَا رَسُولُ اللهِ صَلَّى اللهُ عَلَيْهِ وَسَلَّمَ ذَاتَ يَوْمٍ: إِنَّ اللهَ هُوَ السَّلَامُ، فَإِذَا قَعَدَ أَحَدُكُمْ فِي الصَّلَاةِ فَلْيَقُلْ: التَّحِيَّاتُ لِلّٰهِ وَالصَّلَوَاتُ وَالطَّيِّبَاتُ، السَّلَامُ عَلَيْكَ أَيُّهَا النَّبِيُّ وَرَحْمَةُ اللهِ وَبَرَكَاتُهُ، السَّلَامُ عَلَيْنَا وَعَلَى عِبَادِ اللهِ الصَّالِحِينَ، فَإِذَا قَالَهَا أَصَابَتْ كُلَّ عَبْدٍ لِلّٰهِ صَالِحٍ فِي السَّمَاءِ وَالْأَرْضِ، أَشْهَدُ أَنْ لَا إِلَهَ إِلَّا اللهُ وَأَشْهَدُ أَنَّ مُحَمَّدًا عَبْدُهُ وَرَسُولُهُ، ثُمَّ يَتَخَيَّرُ مِنَ الْمَسْأَلَةِ مَا شَاءَ.

During the prayer, we would say behing the Messenger of Allah ﷺ, 'Peace be upon Allah, peace be upon so and so. . .' Then one day the Messenger of Allah ﷺ told us, 'Allah Himself is peace, so when any one of you sits during the prayer, he should say, "Greetings are for Allah, as well as all prayers and all good things. Peace be upon you, O Prophet, and Allah's mercy and blessings. Peace be upon us and Allah's righteous slaves." When he says this, it reaches every righteous slave of Allah in heaven and on Earth. "I testify that there is no god but Allah, and I testify that Muḥammad is His slave and Messenger." Then he may choose to ask what he wishes.'

35. THE COMPANIONS ASKED THE PROPHET ﷺ, 'WE KNOW HOW TO GREET YOU WITH PEACE. . .

خَرَجَ عَلَيْنَا فَقُلْنَا: يَا رَسُولَ اللهِ قَدْ عَلِمْنَا كَيْفَ نُسَلِّمُ عَلَيْكَ فَكَيْفَ نُصَلِّي عَلَيْكَ؟ قَالَ: فَقُولُوا: اللَّهُمَّ صَلِّ عَلَى مُحَمَّدٍ وَعَلَى آلِ مُحَمَّدٍ كَمَا صَلَّيْتَ عَلَى آلِ إِبْرَاهِيمَ إِنَّكَ حَمِيدٌ مَجِيدٌ، اللَّهُمَّ بَارِكْ عَلَى مُحَمَّدٍ وَعَلَى آلِ مُحَمَّدٍ كَمَا بَارَكْتَ عَلَى آلِ إِبْرَاهِيمَ إِنَّكَ حَمِيدٌ مَجِيدٌ.

When he ﷺ came out to us we asked, 'O Messenger of Allah, we know how to greet you with peace, but how do we invoke blessings upon you?' He said, 'Say: "O Allah, bless Muḥammad and the family of Muḥammad like you blessed the family of Ibrāhīm. O Allah, give increase to Muḥammad and the family of Muḥammad like you gave increase to the family of Ibrāhīm. Truly you are Praiseworthy and Majestic."'

58. 'INDEED, ONE OF YOU DOES THE DEEDS OF THE PEOPLE OF PARADISE. . .

فَإِنَّ أَحَدَكُمْ لَيَعْمَلُ بِعَمَلِ أَهْلِ الْجَنَّةِ حَتَّى مَا يَكُونُ بَيْنَهُ وَبَيْنَهَا إِلَّا ذِرَاعٌ أَوْ قِيدُ ذِرَاعٍ فَيَسْبِقُ عَلَيْهِ الْكِتَابُ فَيَعْمَلُ بِعَمَلِ أَهْلِ النَّارِ فَيَدْخُلُهَا، وَإِنَّ أَحَدَكُمْ لَيَعْمَلُ بِعَمَلِ أَهْلِ النَّارِ حَتَّى مَا يَكُونُ بَيْنَهُ وَبَيْنَهَا إِلَّا ذِرَاعٌ أَوْ قِيدُ ذِرَاعٍ فَيَسْبِقُ عَلَيْهِ الْكِتَابُ فَيَعْمَلُ بِعَمَلِ أَهْلِ الْجَنَّةِ فَيَدْخُلُهَا.

Indeed, one of you does the deeds of the people of Paradise until there is nothing between him and it except the length of a forearm, then what was written overtakes him and he does the deeds of the people of the Fire and enters it. One of you does the deeds of the people of the Fire until there is nothing between him and it except the length of a forearm, then what was written overtakes him and he does the deeds of the people of Paradise and enters it.

68. THE HADITH OF THE TWO HANDFULS OF THE PROGENY OF ĀDAM

إِنَّ اللّٰهَ تَعَالَى خَلَقَ آدَمَ ثُمَّ مَسَحَ ظَهْرَهُ بِيَمِينِهِ فَاسْتَخْرَجَ مِنْهُ ذُرِّيَّةً، فَقَالَ: خَلَقْتُ هَؤُلَاءِ لِلْجَنَّةِ وَبِعَمَلِ أَهْلِ الْجَنَّةِ يَعْمَلُونَ. ثُمَّ مَسَحَ ظَهْرَهُ فَاسْتَخْرَجَ مِنْهُ ذُرِّيَّةً، فَقَالَ، خَلَقْتُ هَؤُلَاءِ لِلنَّارِ وَبِعَمَلِ أَهْلِ النَّارِ يَعْمَلُونَ.

Truly, Allah ﷻ created Ādam ﷺ then wiped his back with His Right Hand and drew out his offspring from him. He then said, 'I have created these for Paradise and they will do the deeds of the people of Paradise. He ﷻ then wiped his back and drew out his offspring from him and said, 'I have created these for the Fire and they will do the deeds of the inmates of the Fire.'

83. THE STORY OF MĀʿIZ ﷺ, WHO COMMITTED ADULTERY AND WAS STONED

جَاءَ مَاعِزُ بْنُ مَالِكٍ إِلَى النَّبِيِّ صَلَّى اللهُ عَلَيْهِ وَسَلَّمَ فَقَالَ: يَا رَسُولَ اللهِ طَهِّرْنِي! فَقَالَ: وَيْحَكَ! ارْجِعْ فَاسْتَغْفِرْ اللهَ وَتُبْ إِلَيْهِ! قَالَ: فَرَجَعَ غَيْرَ بَعِيدٍ ثُمَّ جَاءَ فَقَالَ: يَا رَسُولَ اللهِ طَهِّرْنِي! فَقَالَ رَسُولُ اللهِ صَلَّى اللهُ عَلَيْهِ وَسَلَّمَ: وَيْحَكَ! ارْجِعْ فَاسْتَغْفِرْ اللهَ وَتُبْ إِلَيْهِ! قَالَ: فَرَجَعَ غَيْرَ بَعِيدٍ ثُمَّ جَاءَ فَقَالَ: يَا رَسُولَ اللهِ طَهِّرْنِي! فَقَالَ النَّبِيُّ صَلَّى اللهُ عَلَيْهِ وَسَلَّمَ مِثْلَ ذَلِكَ، حَتَّى إِذَا كَانَتْ الرَّابِعَةُ قَالَ لَهُ رَسُولُ اللهِ: فِيمَ أُطَهِّرُكَ؟ فَقَالَ: مِنْ الزِّنَى. فَسَأَلَ رَسُولُ اللهِ صَلَّى اللهُ عَلَيْهِ وَسَلَّمَ: أَبِهِ جُنُونٌ؟ فَأُخْبِرَ أَنَّهُ لَيْسَ بِمَجْنُونٍ، فَقَالَ: أَشَرِبَ خَمْرًا؟ فَقَامَ رَجُلٌ فَاسْتَنْكَهَهُ فَلَمْ يَجِدْ مِنْهُ رِيحَ خَمْرٍ. قَالَ: فَقَالَ رَسُولُ اللهِ صَلَّى اللهُ عَلَيْهِ وَسَلَّمَ: أَزَنَيْتَ؟ فَقَالَ: نَعَمْ. فَأَمَرَ بِهِ فَرُجِمَ. فَكَانَ النَّاسُ فِيهِ فِرْقَتَيْنِ، قَائِلٌ يَقُولُ لَقَدْ هَلَكَ لَقَدْ أَحَاطَتْ بِهِ خَطِيئَتُهُ، وَقَائِلٌ يَقُولُ مَا تَوْبَةٌ أَفْضَلَ مِنْ تَوْبَةِ مَاعِزٍ أَنَّهُ جَاءَ إِلَى النَّبِيِّ صَلَّى اللهُ عَلَيْهِ وَسَلَّمَ فَوَضَعَ يَدَهُ فِي يَدِهِ ثُمَّ قَالَ: اقْتُلْنِي بِالْحِجَارَةِ. قَالَ: فَلَبِثُوا بِذَلِكَ يَوْمَيْنِ أَوْ ثَلَاثَةً ثُمَّ جَاءَ رَسُولُ اللهِ صَلَّى اللهُ عَلَيْهِ وَسَلَّمَ وَهُمْ جُلُوسٌ فَسَلَّمَ ثُمَّ جَلَسَ فَقَالَ: اسْتَغْفِرُوا لِمَاعِزِ بْنِ مَالِكٍ. قَالَ: فَقَالُوا: غَفَرَ اللهُ لِمَاعِزِ بْنِ مَالِكٍ. قَالَ:

فَقَالَ رَسُولُ اللهِ صَلَّى اللهُ عَلَيْهِ وَسَلَّمَ: لَقَدْ تَابَ تَوْبَةً لَوْ قُسِمَتْ بَيْنَ أُمَّةٍ لَوَسِعَتْهُمْ.

Māʿiz ibn Mālik came to the Prophet ﷺ and said to him, 'O Messenger of Allah, purify me!' The Prophet said, 'Woe to you! Go back, seek Allah's forgiveness and repent to Him.' It was not long before he returned and said, 'O Messenger of Allah, purify me!' So the Prophet said, 'Woe to you! Go back, seek Allah's forgiveness and repent to Him.' Then he came and said, 'O Messenger of Allah, purify me!' The Prophet ﷺ replied the same until Māʿiz came back for the fourth time. Allah's Messenger ﷺ then said to him, 'What am I purifying you from?' So he said, 'From adultery.' Allah's Messenger asked, 'Is he crazy?' and he was informed that he was not crazy. He said, 'Has he been drinking wine?' So a man stood up, checked his breath and did not find the smell of wine. Allah's Messenger ﷺ said, 'Have you committed adultery?' He said, 'Yes.' So the Prophet ordered that he be stoned. Thereafter, people were in two groups concerning him. One would say, 'He has been destroyed, his sin has encompassed him.' Another would say, 'There is no repentance better than the repentance of Māʿiz. He came to the Prophet ﷺ, placed his hand in his hand, then said to him, "Kill me with stones."' So the people continued to say this for two or three days, until Allah's Messenger ﷺ came to them while they were sitting. He greeted them, sat down and said, 'Seek forgiveness for Māʿiz ibn Mālik.' So they said, 'May Allah forgive Māʿiz ibn Mālik.' Allah's Messenger ﷺ said, 'He has repented with a repentance that, if it were divided, could suffice a nation.'

84. THE PROHIBITION OF INTERCEDING ABOUT A PRESCRIBED PUNISHMENT WHEN THE MATTER HAS REACHED THE RULER

أَنَّ قُرَيْشًا أَهَمَّتْهُمْ الْمَرْأَةُ الْمَخْزُومِيَّةُ الَّتِي سَرَقَتْ، فَقَالُوا: مَنْ يُكَلِّمُ رَسُولَ اللهِ صَلَّى اللهُ عَلَيْهِ وَسَلَّمَ؟ وَمَنْ يَجْتَرِئُ عَلَيْهِ إِلَّا أُسَامَةُ بْنُ زَيْدٍ حِبُّ رَسُولِ اللهِ صَلَّى اللهُ عَلَيْهِ وَسَلَّمَ؟ فَكَلَّمَ رَسُولَ اللهِ صَلَّى اللهُ عَلَيْهِ وَسَلَّمَ فَقَالَ: أَتَشْفَعُ فِي حَدٍّ مِنْ حُدُودِ اللهِ؟ ثُمَّ قَامَ فَخَطَبَ، قَالَ: يَا أَيُّهَا النَّاسُ! إِنَّمَا ضَلَّ مَنْ قَبْلَكُمْ أَنَّهُمْ كَانُوا إِذَا سَرَقَ الشَّرِيفُ تَرَكُوهُ وَإِذَا سَرَقَ الضَّعِيفُ فِيهِمْ أَقَامُوا عَلَيْهِ الْحَدَّ. وَايْمُ اللهِ لَوْ أَنَّ فَاطِمَةَ بِنْتَ مُحَمَّدٍ صَلَّى اللهُ عَلَيْهِ وَسَلَّمَ سَرَقَتْ لَقَطَعَ مُحَمَّدٌ يَدَهَا!

The Quraysh were concerned about the affair of a Makhzūmī woman who had stolen. They said, 'Who will speak to Allah's Messenger ﷺ on her behalf? None would dare do so except Usāmah ibn Zayd, he is the beloved of Allah's Messenger.' So Usāmah spoke with him. Allah's Messenger ﷺ said, 'Do you intercede concerning one of Allah's prescribed punishments?!' He then stood and delivered a sermon: 'O people! Truly, what destroyed those before you is that whenever a noble person among them stole, they left him; but when a weak person stole, they implemented the punishment on him. By Allah, if Fāṭimah, the daughter of Muḥammad, stole, I would surely cut her hand off!'

96. THE HADITH OF THE NOCTURNAL JOURNEY

أُتِيتُ بِالْبُرَاقِ وَهُوَ دَابَّةٌ أَبْيَضُ فَوْقَ الْحِمَارِ وَدُونَ الْبَغْلِ يَضَعُ حَافِرَهُ عِنْدَ مُنْتَهَى طَرَفِهِ، فَرَكِبْتُهُ فَسَارَ بِي حَتَّى أَتَيْت بَيْتَ الْمَقْدِسِ فَرَبَطْتُ الدَّابَّةَ

بِالْحَلَقَةِ الَّتِي كَانَ يَرْبِطُ بِهَا الْأَنْبِيَاءُ، ثُمَّ دَخَلْتُ فَصَلَّيْتُ فِيهِ رَكْعَتَيْنِ، ثُمَّ خَرَجْتُ فَجَاءَنِي جِبْرِيلُ بِإِنَاءٍ مِنْ خَمْرٍ وَإِنَاءٍ مِنْ لَبَنٍ، فَاخْتَرْتُ اللَّبَنَ، فَقَالَ جِبْرِيلُ: أَصَبْتَ الْفِطْرَةَ. قَالَ: ثُمَّ عَرَجَ بِنَا إِلَى السَّمَاءِ الدُّنْيَا فَاسْتَفْتَحَ جِبْرِيلُ فَقِيلَ: مَنْ أَنْتَ؟ فَقَالَ: جِبْرِيلُ. قِيلَ: وَمَنْ مَعَكَ؟ قَالَ: مُحَمَّدٌ. فَقِيلَ: وَقَدْ أُرْسِلَ إِلَيْهِ؟ فَقَالَ: قَدْ أُرْسِلَ إِلَيْهِ. فَفَتَحَ لَنَا فَإِذَا أَنَا بِآدَمَ فَرَحَّبَ وَدَعَا لِي بِخَيْرٍ، ثُمَّ عَرَجَ بِنَا إِلَى السَّمَاءِ الثَّانِيَةِ فَاسْتَفْتَحَ جِبْرِيلُ فَقِيلَ: وَمَنْ أَنْتَ؟ قَالَ: جِبْرِيلُ. فَقِيلَ: وَمَنْ مَعَكَ؟ قَالَ: مُحَمَّدٌ. فَقِيلَ: وَقَدْ أُرْسِلَ إِلَيْهِ؟ قَالَ: قَدْ أُرْسِلَ إِلَيْهِ. فَفَتَحَ لَنَا فَإِذَا أَنَا بِابْنَيْ الْخَالَةِ يَحْيَى وَعِيسَى فَرَحَّبَا وَدَعَوَا لِي بِخَيْرٍ، ثُمَّ عَرَجَ بِنَا إِلَى السَّمَاءِ الثَّالِثَةِ فَاسْتَفْتَحَ جِبْرِيلُ فَقِيلَ: وَمَنْ أَنْتَ؟ فَقَالَ: جِبْرِيلُ. فَقِيلَ: وَمَنْ مَعَكَ؟ قَالَ: مُحَمَّدٌ. قَالُوا: وَقَدْ أُرْسِلَ إِلَيْهِ؟ قَالَ: قَدْ أُرْسِلَ إِلَيْهِ. فَفَتَحَ لَنَا فَإِذَا أَنَا بِيُوسُفَ وَإِذَا هُوَ قَدْ أُعْطِيَ شَطْرَ الْحُسْنِ فَرَحَّبَ وَدَعَا لِي بِخَيْرٍ، ثُمَّ عَرَجَ بِنَا إِلَى السَّمَاءِ الرَّابِعَةِ فَاسْتَفْتَحَ جِبْرِيلُ فَقِيلَ: وَمَنْ أَنْتَ؟ فَقَالَ: جِبْرِيلُ. فَقِيلَ: وَمَنْ مَعَكَ؟ قَالَ: مُحَمَّدٌ صَلَّى اللهُ عَلَيْهِ وَسَلَّمَ. فَقِيلَ: وَقَدْ أُرْسِلَ إِلَيْهِ؟ فَقَالَ: قَدْ أُرْسِلَ إِلَيْهِ. فَفَتَحَ لَنَا فَإِذَا أَنَا بِإِدْرِيسَ فَرَحَّبَ وَدَعَا لِي بِخَيْرٍ، ثُمَّ قَالَ: يَقُولُ اللهُ: ﴿وَرَفَعْنَاهُ مَكَانًا عَلِيًّا﴾ ثُمَّ عَرَجَ بِنَا إِلَى السَّمَاءِ الْخَامِسَةِ فَاسْتَفْتَحَ جِبْرِيلُ فَقِيلَ: مَنْ أَنْتَ؟ قَالَ: جِبْرِيلُ. فَقِيلَ: وَمَنْ مَعَكَ؟ فَقَالَ: مُحَمَّدٌ. فَقِيلَ: وَقَدْ بُعِثَ إِلَيْهِ؟ قَالَ: قَدْ بُعِثَ إِلَيْهِ. فَفَتَحَ لَنَا فَإِذَا أَنَا بِهَارُونَ فَرَحَّبَ بِي وَدَعَا لِي بِخَيْرٍ، ثُمَّ عَرَجَ بِنَا إِلَى السَّمَاءِ السَّادِسَةِ فَاسْتَفْتَحَ جِبْرِيلُ فَقِيلَ: مَنْ أَنْتَ؟ قَالَ: جِبْرِيلُ. فَقِيلَ: وَمَنْ مَعَكَ؟ قَالَ مُحَمَّدٌ. فَقِيلَ: وَقَدْ بُعِثَ إِلَيْهِ؟ قَالَ: قَدْ بُعِثَ إِلَيْهِ. فَفَتَحَ لَنَا فَإِذَا أَنَا بِمُوسَى

فَرَحَّبَ وَدَعَا لِي بِخَيْرٍ، ثُمَّ عَرَجَ بِنَا إِلَى السَّمَاءِ السَّابِعَةِ فَاسْتَفْتَحَ جِبْرِيلُ فَقِيلَ: مَنْ أَنْتَ؟ قَالَ: جِبْرِيلُ. فَقِيلَ: وَمَنْ مَعَك؟ قَالَ :مُحَمَّدٌ. فَقِيلَ: وَقَدْ بُعِثَ إِلَيْهِ؟ قَالَ: قَدْ بُعِثَ إِلَيْهِ. فَفَتَحَ لَنَا فَإِذَا أَنَا بِإِبْرَاهِيمَ وَإِذَا هُوَ مُسْنِدٌ إِلَى الْبَيْتِ الْمَعْمُورِ، وَإِذَا هُوَ يَدْخُلُهُ كُلَّ يَوْمٍ سَبْعُونَ أَلْفَ مَلَكٍ لَا يَعُودُونَ إِلَيْهِ. ثُمَّ ذَهَبَ بِي إِلَى سِدْرَةِ الْمُنْتَهَى فَإِذَا وَرَقُهَا كَآذَانِ الْفِيَلَةِ وَإِذَا ثَمَرُهَا أَمْثَالُ الْقِلَالِ، فَلَمَّا غَشِيَهَا مِنْ أَمْرِ اللهِ مَا غَشِيَهَا تَغَيَّرَتْ، فَمَا أَحَدٌ مِنْ خَلْقِ اللهِ يَسْتَطِيعُ أَنْ يَصِفَهَا مِنْ حُسْنِهَا. قَالَ: فَأَوْحَى اللهُ إِلَيَّ مَا أَوْحَى وَفَرَضَ عَلَيَّ فِي كُلِّ يَوْمٍ وَلَيْلَةٍ خَمْسِينَ صَلَاةً. فَنَزَلْتُ حَتَّى انْتَهَيْتُ إِلَى مُوسَى فَقَالَ: مَا فَرَضَ رَبُّك عَلَى أُمَّتِك؟ قَالَ: قُلْت: خَمْسِينَ صَلَاةً فِي كُلِّ يَوْمٍ وَلَيْلَةٍ. فَقَالَ: ارْجِعْ إِلَى رَبِّك فَاسْأَلْهُ التَّخْفِيفَ فَإِنَّ أُمَّتَك لَا تُطِيقُ ذَلِكَ، فَإِنِّي قَدْ بَلَوْتُ بَنِي إِسْرَائِيلَ وَخَبَرْتُهُمْ. قَالَ: فَرَجَعْتُ إِلَى رَبِّي فَقُلْتُ لَهُ: رَبِّ خَفِّفْ عَنْ أُمَّتِي. فَحَطَّ عَنِّي خَمْسًا فَرَجَعْتُ إِلَى مُوسَى فَقَالَ: مَا فَعَلْتَ؟ فَقُلْتُ: حَطَّ عَنِّي خَمْسًا. قَالَ: إِنَّ أُمَّتَك لَا تُطِيقُ ذَلِكَ، فَارْجِعْ إِلَى رَبِّك فَاسْأَلْهُ التَّخْفِيفَ لِأُمَّتِك. فَلَمْ أَزَلْ أَرْجِعُ بَيْنَ رَبِّي وَبَيْنَ مُوسَى عَلَيْهِ السَّلَامُ فَيَحُطُّ عَنِّي خَمْسًا خَمْسًا حَتَّى قَالَ: يَا مُحَمَّدُ هِيَ خَمْسُ صَلَوَاتٍ فِي كُلِّ يَوْمٍ وَلَيْلَةٍ، بِكُلِّ صَلَاةٍ عَشْرٌ فَتِلْكَ خَمْسُونَ صَلَاةً، وَمَنْ هَمَّ بِحَسَنَةٍ فَلَمْ يَعْمَلْهَا كُتِبَتْ لَهُ حَسَنَةً فَإِنْ عَمِلَهَا كُتِبَتْ لَهُ عَشْرًا، وَمَنْ هَمَّ بِسَيِّئَةٍ وَلَمْ يَعْمَلْهَا لَمْ تُكْتَبْ لَهُ شَيْئًا، فَإِنْ عَمِلَهَا كُتِبَتْ سَيِّئَةً وَاحِدَةً. فَنَزَلْتُ حَتَّى انْتَهَيْتُ إِلَى مُوسَى فَأَخْبَرْتُهُ فَقَالَ: ارْجِعْ إِلَى رَبِّك فَاسْأَلْهُ التَّخْفِيفَ لِأُمَّتِك فَإِنَّ أُمَّتَك لَا تُطِيقُ ذَلِكَ. فَقَالَ رَسُولُ اللهِ صَلَّى اللهُ عَلَيْهِ وَسَلَّمَ: لَقَدْ رَجَعْتُ إِلَى رَبِّي حَتَّى اسْتَحْيَيْتُ.

[Allah's Messenger ﷺ said:] Burāq was brought to me—a tall, white animal, bigger than a donkey but smaller than a mule, that places its hoof to the extent of its vision. I rode it until I was brought to Jerusalem, and tied it with the harness that the prophets use to tie. Then I entered the mosque and prayed two units of prayer therein. I exited and Jibrīl ﷺ came to me with a vessel of wine and a vessel of milk. I chose the milk. Jibrīl ﷺ said, 'You chose the natural thing.' Then he took us up to heaven and sought permission to enter. It was said, 'Who are you?' He said, 'Jibrīl.' It was said, 'And who is with you?"' He said, 'Muḥammad.' It was said, 'Has he been sent for?' He said, 'He has been sent for.' So it was opened for us, and low and behold I was with Ādam ﷺ. He welcomed me and prayed for me to receive goodness. Then he took us up to the second heaven and sought permission to enter. It was said, 'Who are you?' He said, 'Jibrīl.' It was said, 'And who is with you?' He said, 'Muḥammad.' It was said, 'Has he been sent for?' He said, 'He has been sent for.' So it was opened for us, and low and behold I was with the two cousins, 'Īsā [the son of Maryam] and Yaḥyā [the son of Zakariyyah] ﷺ. They welcomed me and prayed for me to receive goodness. Then he took us up to the third heaven and sought permission to enter. It was said, 'Who are you?' He said, 'Jibrīl.' It was said, 'And who is with you?' He said, 'Muḥammad.' It was said, 'Has he been sent for?' He said, 'He has been sent for.' So it was opened for us, and low and behold I was with Yūsuf ﷺ, who was given half of beauty. He greeted me and prayed for me to receive goodness. Then he took us up to the fourth heaven and sought permission to enter. It was said, 'Who is it?' He said, 'Jibrīl.' It was said, 'And who is with you? He said, 'Muḥammad.' It was said, 'Has he been sent for?' He said, 'He has been sent for.' So it was opened for us, and low and behold I was with Idrīs ﷺ. He welcomed me and prayed for me to receive goodness. Allah ﷻ said, '*We raised him to a lofty place.*'

Then he took us up to the fifth heaven and sought permission to enter. It was said, 'Who is it?' He said, 'Jibrīl.' It was said, 'And who is with you?' He said, 'Muḥammad.' It was said, 'Has he been sent for?' He said, 'He has been sent for.' So it was opened for us, and low and behold I was with Hārūn ﷺ. He welcomed me and prayed for me to receive goodness. Then he took us up to the sixth heaven and sought permission to enter. It was said, 'Who is it?' He said, 'Jibrīl.' It was said, 'And who is with you?' He said, 'Muḥammad.' It was said, 'Has he been sent for?' He said, 'He has been sent for.' So it was opened for us, and low and behold I was with Mūsā ﷺ. He welcomed me and prayed for me to receive goodness. Then he took us up to the seventh heaven and sought permission to enter. It was said, 'Who is it?' He said, 'Jibrīl.' It was said, 'And who is with you?' He said, 'Muḥammad.' It was said, 'Has he been sent for?' He said, 'He has been sent for.' So it was opened for us, and low and behold I was with Ibrāhīm ﷺ. He was sitting with his back against the wall of Bayt al-Maʿmūr, to which 70,00. angels enter daily and do not return to it. Then Jibrīl went with me to the Furthest Lotus Tree. Its leaves are like elephant ears and its fruits like huge jars. It changed when there came whatever came to it from Allah's command. No one from Allah's creation can describe its beauty. Allah revealed to me what he revealed to me, and obligated upon me fifty prayers every day and night. I went down to Mūsā ﷺ and he said, 'What did your Lord obligate upon your community?' I said, 'Fifty prayers.' He said, 'Go back to your Lord and ask for less, for truly your community is not able to do that. I know this from my experience with the Children of Isrā'īl.' So I went back to my Lord and said, 'O Lord! Lighten the burden on my community.' So five were decreased. I returned to Mūsā and said, 'Five were decreased.' He said, 'Truly, your community is not able to do that. Go back to your Lord and ask for less.' So I did not stop going back between my Lord ﷻ and Mūsā ﵇ until He said, 'O Muḥammad! Indeed, they are five prayers every day and night, and for every prayer is the reward of ten; that will be fifty prayers. Whoever plans to undertake a good deed yet does not do it, a good deed is written for him. If he does it, then he has the reward of ten. Whoever plans to commit a bad deed and does not do it, nothing is written against him. If he does it, one bad deed is written against him.' So I went down until I reached Mūsā ﵇ and informed him. He said, 'Go back to your Lord and ask for less.' I said, 'I have already gone back to Him to the point that now I feel too shy.'

97. THE HADITH OF THE CAMEL THAT COMPLAINED TO THE PROPHET ﷺ ABOUT ITS OWNER.

كَانَ أَهْلُ بَيْتٍ مِنَ الْأَنْصَارِ لَهُمْ جَمَلٌ يَسْنُونَ عَلَيْهِ. وَإِنَّ الْجَمَلَ اسْتُصْعِبَ عَلَيْهِمْ فَمَنَعَهُمْ ظَهْرَهُ، وَإِنَّ الْأَنْصَارَ جَاءُوا إِلَى رَسُولِ اللهِ صَلَّى اللهُ عَلَيْهِ وَسَلَّمَ فَقَالُوا: إِنَّهُ كَانَ لَنَا جَمَلٌ نُسْنِي عَلَيْهِ وَإِنَّهُ اسْتُصْعِبَ عَلَيْنَا وَمَنَعَنَا ظَهْرَهُ وَقَدْ عَطِشَ الزَّرْعُ وَالنَّخْلُ. فَقَالَ رَسُولُ اللهِ صَلَّى اللهُ عَلَيْهِ وَسَلَّمَ لِأَصْحَابِهِ: قُومُوا! فَقَامُوا فَدَخَلَ الْحَائِطَ وَالْجَمَلُ فِي نَاحِيَةٍ، فَمَشَى النَّبِيُّ صَلَّى اللهُ عَلَيْهِ وَسَلَّمَ نَحْوَهُ فَقَالَتِ الْأَنْصَارُ: يَا نَبِيَّ اللهِ، إِنَّهُ قَدْ صَارَ مِثْلَ الْكَلْبِ وَإِنَّا نَخَافُ عَلَيْكَ صَوْلَتَهُ. فَقَالَ: لَيْسَ عَلَيَّ مِنْهُ بَأْسٌ. فَلَمَّا نَظَرَ الْجَمَلُ إِلَى رَسُولِ اللهِ صَلَّى اللهُ عَلَيْهِ وَسَلَّمَ أَقْبَلَ نَحْوَهُ حَتَّى خَرَّ سَاجِدًا بَيْنَ يَدَيْهِ فَأَخَذَ رَسُولُ اللهِ صَلَّى اللهُ عَلَيْهِ وَسَلَّمَ بِنَاصِيَتِهِ أَذَلَّ مَا كَانَتْ قَطُّ حَتَّى أَدْخَلَهُ فِي الْعَمَلِ، فَقَالَ لَهُ أَصْحَابُهُ: يَا رَسُولَ اللهِ،

هَذِهِ بَهِيمَةٌ لَا تَعْقِلُ تَسْجُدُ لَكَ وَنَحْنُ نَعْقِلُ فَنَحْنُ أَحَقُّ أَنْ نَسْجُدَ لَكَ: فَقَالَ: لَا يَصْلُحُ لِبَشَرٍ أَنْ يَسْجُدَ لِبَشَرٍ، وَلَوْ صَلَحَ لِبَشَرٍ أَنْ يَسْجُدَ لِبَشَرٍ لَأَمَرْتُ الْمَرْأَةَ أَنْ تَسْجُدَ لِزَوْجِهَا مِنْ عِظَمِ حَقِّهِ عَلَيْهَا. وَالَّذِي نَفْسِي بِيَدِهِ لَوْ كَانَ مِنْ قَدَمِهِ إِلَى مَفْرِقِ رَأْسِهِ قُرْحَةً تَنْبَجِسُ بِالْقَيْحِ وَالصَّدِيدِ ثُمَّ اسْتَقْبَلَتْهُ فَلَحَسَتْهُ مَا أَدَّتْ حَقَّهُ.

A household from the Helpers (Anṣār) had a camel which they used to ride to collect water. The camel became difficult towards them and refused to let them mount it, so the Helpers came to the Messenger of Allah ﷺ and said, 'We had a camel that we used to ride to collect water, but it has become difficult towards us and refuses to let us mount it. Now the crops and palms are thirsty.' The Messenger of Allah ﷺ said to his Companions, 'Get up!' So they got up and entered the enclosure on one side of which was the camel. The Prophet ﷺ walked in its direction and the Helpers said, 'O Prophet of Allah, it has become like a dog and we fear that it will attack you!' He replied, 'It will do me no harm.' When the camel looked at the Messenger of Allah ﷺ, it approached him until it sank prostrate before him. Then the Messenger of Allah ﷺ took it by the forelock, as docile as it had ever been, and set it to work. His Companions said to him, 'O Messenger of Allah ﷺ, this is a beast without reason and it prostrates to you. We have reason, so we are even more obligated to prostrate to you.' He replied, 'It is not right for any person to prostrate to another person. If it were right for a person to prostrate to another person, I would have ordered every woman to prostrate to her husband, due to the magnitude of his right upon her. By the One in Whose Hand is my soul, if he were covered from head to toe in suppurating ulcers, and she came and licked them clean, she still would not have fulfilled his right.'

98. THE HADITH OF THE TREE STUMP LONGING FOR THE PROPHET ﷺ

أَنَّ رَسُولَ اللهِ صَلَّى اللهُ عَلَيْهِ وَسَلَّمَ كَانَ يَخْطُبُ إِلَى جِذْعٍ، فَلَمَّا اتَّخَذَ الْمِنْبَرَ تَحَوَّلَ إِلَيْهِ فَحَنَّ الْجِذْعُ، فَأَتَى النَّبِيُّ صَلَّى اللهُ عَلَيْهِ وَسَلَّمَ فَمَسَحَهُ.

The Messenger of Allah ﷺ would deliver sermons leaning against a tree stump. When he adopted the pulpit, he used it instead. The tree stump yearned for him, so the Prophet ﷺ came and wiped his hands over it.

99. 'I WAS GIVEN FIVE THINGS. . .'

أُعْطِيتُ خَمْسًا لَمْ يُعْطَهُنَّ أَحَدٌ مِنَ الْأَنْبِيَاءِ قَبْلِي: نُصِرْتُ بِالرُّعْبِ مَسِيرَةَ شَهْرٍ، وَجُعِلَتْ لِي الْأَرْضُ مَسْجِدًا وَطَهُورًا فَأَيُّمَا رَجُلٌ مِنْ أُمَّتِي أَدْرَكَتْهُ الصَّلَاةُ فَلْيُصَلِّ، وَأُحِلَّتْ لِي الْمَغَانِمُ وَلَمْ تَحِلَّ لِأَحَدٍ قَبْلِي، وَأُعْطِيتُ الشَّفَاعَةَ، وَكَانَ النَّبِيُّ يُبْعَثُ إِلَى قَوْمِهِ خَاصَّةً وَبُعِثْتُ إِلَى النَّاسِ عَامَّةً.

[The Prophet ﷺ said:] I was given five things that no prophet before me was given: I was made victorious through awe reaching a month's distance; the Earth was made a pure mosque for me, so if the time of prayer comes upon anyone from my community he may pray anywhere; the spoils of war were made lawful for me while they were not lawful for anyone before me; I have been granted intercession; and prophets were sent specifically to their respective peoples, yet I have been sent to all people in general.

109. THE HADITH OF THE QUESTIONING OF THE DECEASED IN HIS GRAVE

الْعَبْدُ إِذَا وُضِعَ فِي قَبْرِهِ وَتُوُلِّيَ وَذَهَبَ أَصْحَابُهُ حَتَّى إِنَّهُ لَيَسْمَعُ قَرْعَ نِعَالِهِمْ أَتَاهُ مَلَكَانِ فَأَقْعَدَاهُ فَيَقُولَانِ لَهُ: مَا كُنْتَ تَقُولُ فِي هَذَا الرَّجُلِ مُحَمَّدٍ صَلَّى اللهُ عَلَيْهِ وَسَلَّمَ؟ فَيَقُولُ: أَشْهَدُ أَنَّهُ عَبْدُ اللهِ وَرَسُولُهُ. فَيُقَالُ: انْظُرْ إِلَى مَقْعَدِكَ مِنَ النَّارِ أَبْدَلَكَ اللهُ بِهِ مَقْعَدًا مِنَ الْجَنَّةِ. قَالَ النَّبِيُّ صَلَّى اللهُ عَلَيْهِ وَسَلَّمَ: فَيَرَاهُمَا جَمِيعًا. وَأَمَّا الْكَافِرُ أَوْ الْمُنَافِقُ فَيَقُولُ: لَا أَدْرِي! كُنْتُ أَقُولُ مَا يَقُولُ النَّاسُ! فَيُقَالُ: لَا دَرَيْتَ وَلَا تَلَيْتَ! ثُمَّ يُضْرَبُ بِمِطْرَقَةٍ مِنْ حَدِيدٍ ضَرْبَةً بَيْنَ أُذُنَيْهِ، فَيَصِيحُ صَيْحَةً يَسْمَعُهَا مَنْ يَلِيهِ إِلَّا الثَّقَلَيْنِ.

[Allah's Prophet ﷺ said:] Truly, when the slave is put in his grave and his companions go away and he hears the beating of their sandals, two angels come to him, sit him up, and say to him, 'What did you used to say about this man, Muhammad ﷺ?' He will say, 'I testify that he is Allah's slave and Messenger.' It will then be said, 'Look at your place in the Fire. Allah has replaced it for you with a place in Paradise.'

The Prophet ﷺ said: He will see both of them. As for the unbeliever or the hypocrite, he will say, 'I do not know! I used to say what the people said!' He will then be told, 'You have not understood, nor followed correctly!' Then he will be struck with an iron hammer between his ears and he will cry out such a cry which is heard by all those close by except Man and Jinn.

110. THE HADITH OF THE BASIN

إِنِّي فَرَطُكُمْ عَلَى الْحَوْضِ. مَنْ مَرَّ عَلَيَّ شَرِبَ وَمَنْ شَرِبَ لَمْ يَظْمَأْ أَبَدًا. لَيَرِدَنَّ عَلَيَّ أَقْوَامٌ أَعْرِفُهُمْ وَيَعْرِفُونِي ثُمَّ يُحَالُ بَيْنِي وَبَيْنَهُمْ.

I will be your predecessor at the Basin. Whoever passes by me shall drink and whoever drinks shall never again feel thirsty. There will surely be people who pass by me whom I will recognise and they will recognise me, but they will be blocked from me.

112. THE LONG HADITH OF INTERCESSION AND PEOPLE'S SEEKING IT FROM ONE PROPHET TO ANOTHER.

يَجْتَمِعُ الْمُؤْمِنُونَ يَوْمَ الْقِيَامَةِ فَيَقُولُونَ: لَوِ اسْتَشْفَعْنَا إِلَى رَبِّنَا! فَيَأْتُونَ آدَمَ فَيَقُولُونَ: أَنْتَ أَبُو النَّاسِ، خَلَقَكَ اللهُ بِيَدِهِ وَأَسْجَدَ لَكَ مَلَائِكَتَهُ وَعَلَّمَكَ أَسْمَاءَ كُلِّ شَيْءٍ، فَاشْفَعْ لَنَا عِنْدَ رَبِّكَ حَتَّى يُرِيحَنَا مِنْ مَكَانِنَا هَذَا. فَيَقُولُ: لَسْتُ هُنَاكُمْ، وَيَذْكُرُ ذَنْبَهُ فَيَسْتَحْيِي. ائْتُوا نُوحًا فَإِنَّهُ أَوَّلُ رَسُولٍ بَعَثَهُ اللهُ إِلَى أَهْلِ الْأَرْضِ. فَيَأْتُونَهُ فَيَقُولُ: لَسْتُ هُنَاكُمْ، وَيَذْكُرُ سُؤَالَهُ رَبَّهُ مَا لَيْسَ لَهُ بِهِ عِلْمٌ فَيَسْتَحْيِي. فَيَقُولُ: ائْتُوا خَلِيلَ الرَّحْمَنِ، فَيَأْتُونَهُ، فَيَقُولُ: لَسْتُ هُنَاكُمْ، فَيَقُولُ: ائْتُوا مُوسَى عَبْدًا كَلَّمَهُ اللهُ وَأَعْطَاهُ التَّوْرَاةَ. فَيَأْتُونَهُ، فَيَقُولُ: لَسْتُ هُنَاكُمْ، وَيَذْكُرُ قَتْلَ النَّفْسِ بِغَيْرِ نَفْسٍ، فَيَسْتَحْيِي مِنْ رَبِّهِ، فَيَقُولُ: ائْتُوا عِيسَى عَبْدَ اللهِ وَرَسُولَهُ وَكَلِمَةَ اللهِ وَرُوحَهُ، فَيَأْتُونَهُ، فَيَقُولُ: لَسْتُ هُنَاكُمْ، ائْتُوا مُحَمَّدًا عَبْدًا غَفَرَ اللهُ لَهُ مَا تَقَدَّمَ مِنْ ذَنْبِهِ وَمَا تَأَخَّرَ. فَيَأْتُونِي فَأَنْطَلِقُ حَتَّى

أَسْتَأْذِنَ عَلَى رَبِّي، فَيُؤْذَنُ لِي، فَإِذَا رَأَيْتُ رَبِّي وَقَعْتُ سَاجِدًا فَيَدَعُنِي مَا شَاءَ اللهُ ثُمَّ يُقَالُ: ارْفَعْ رَأْسَكَ، وَسَلْ تُعْطَهُ، وَقُلْ يُسْمَعْ، وَاشْفَعْ تُشَفَّعْ. فَأَرْفَعُ رَأْسِي فَأَحْمَدُهُ بِتَحْمِيدٍ يُعْلِمُنِيهِ ثُمَّ أَشْفَعُ فَيَحُدُّ لِي حَدًّا فَأُدْخِلُهُمُ الْجَنَّةَ، ثُمَّ أَعُودُ إِلَيْهِ، وَإِذَا رَأَيْتُ رَبِّي مِثْلَهُ ثُمَّ أَشْفَعُ فَيَحُدُّ لِي حَدًّا فَأُدْخِلُهُمُ الْجَنَّةَ، ثُمَّ أَعُودُ الرَّابِعَةَ فَأَقُولُ: مَا بَقِيَ فِي النَّارِ إِلَّا مَنْ حَبَسَهُ الْقُرْآنُ وَوَجَبَ عَلَيْهِ الْخُلُودُ.

Believers will be gathered on the Day of Resurrection and they will say, 'If only we sought intercession with our Lord!' So they will go to Ādam ﵇ and say, 'You are the father of all people. Allah created you with His hand, ordered His angels to prostrate to you and taught you the names of all things. Intercede for us with your Lord so that He may relieve us of this place of ours.' He will say, 'I am not the one to do that for you,' and he will mention his shortcoming and feel shame before his Lord due to it and say, 'Rather, go to Nūḥ, the first Messenger that Allah sent.' So they will go to Nūḥ ﵇ and he will say, 'I am not the one to do that for you,' and he will mention that he asked Allah about that which he had no knowledge of and feel shame before his Lord due to it and say, 'Rather, go to Ibrāhīm, he whom Allah took as a dear friend.' So they will go to Ibrahim ﵇ and he will say, 'I am not the one to do that for you. Rather, go to Mūsā, he whom Allah spoke to and gave the Torah.' So they will go to Mūsā ﵇ and he will say, 'I am not the one to do that for you,' and he will mention his killing of a person not in retaliation for the killing of another and feel shame before his Lord because of it and say, 'Rather, go to 'Īsā, the servant of Allah and His messenger, the Spirit of Allah and His Word.' So they will go to 'Īsā ﵇, the Spirit of Allah and His Word ﵇ and he will say, 'I am not the one to do that for you.

Rather, go to Muḥammad, a slave whom Allah has forgiven the first and the last of his shortcomings.' [The Prophet ﷺ then said,] So they will come to me, and I will seek permission from my Lord and He will give me permission. When I see Him, I will fall prostrate. He will leave me like that for however long He wills ﷻ. Then it will be said, 'O Muḥammad! Lift your head! Ask and you will be given, speak and you will be heard, intercede and you will be granted intercession.' So will I lift my head and praise my Lord with words of praise that my Lord will teach me, and then I will intercede. I will be given a limit, so I will bring people out of the Fire and escort them to Paradise. Then I will return to Him and when I see my Lord, the same will happen again. Then I will intercede and be given a limit, so I will bring people out of the Fire and escort them to Paradise. Thereafter I will return for the fourth time and say, 'No one remains in the Fire except he for whom the Qur'ān dictates an eternity therein.'